THE WILDERNESS WAY

This book is set in the typeface *Athelas* designed by Veronika Burian and Jose Scaglione.

Paperback ISBN: 9798391249023

A Publication of *Tall Pine Books*
119 E Center Street, Suite B4A | Warsaw, Indiana 46580
www.tallpinebooks.com

| 1 23 23 20 16 02 |

Published in the United States of America

THE WILDERNESS WAY

THE TRAINING GROUND OF THE WARRIOR

JEREMIAH GIBSON

Dedicated to my daughter Aviel Grace-Glory.

Walking in The Way led us into the valley of the shadow of death, and only your mother and I came out on the other side. We will see you in glory.

For our momentary, light affliction is producing for us an eternal weight of glory far beyond all comparison,
2 Corinthians 4:17

CONTENTS

CONTENTS

INTRODUCTION

Does it feel like you are living in 4D?

Darkness

Depression

Destruction

Death

Called "the desert" by some and "the wilderness" by others, *what is the truth about this place?* Many have gotten lost in the wilderness of this life and never recovered. Maybe you have lived in a place of constant troubles, trials, pressure, and stress, just looking for a way out. The truth is that somehow, some way, and some time in everyone's lives, we will have to traverse a wilderness. Physically, mentally, and spiritually this can be exhausting. Many get lost in this place and are never able to leave.

*But, **what if there was a pathway through the wilderness?***

What if there were a way to walk through the desert that, when followed, would cause you to not just survive but thrive in the harsh outback?

What if the wilderness was a training ground that would strengthen you and cause you to advance through it and into the fullness of your destiny?

What if you could set others free because of what you learned there in "the valley of the shadow of death?"

Abraham walked through the wilderness of barrenness even in the midst of the promise that he would have descendants more numerous than the stars.

Isaac had to walk through the wilderness of uncomfortability, uncertainty, and obedience, beyond reasonable thought, to lay on the altar his father had made.

Jacob had to walk through the wilderness of judgment as a result of his deceptive and manipulative choices as a youth.

Joseph had to walk through the desert of slavery and false accusation.

Moses walked through the wilderness for forty years hiding as an outcast because he tried to deliver his people by his own hand.

David was on the run in the wilderness from the man who was on the throne even after he had been anointed king.

Job walked through the wilderness of loss even though he was a righteous man.

Elijah walked through a wilderness of depression and wanted to die before anointing the next generation to transform the leadership of the nation.

The prophets walked through the valley of a dark-hearted people and were persecuted and outcast for speaking The Truth.

Daniel was cast into the wilderness of Babylon and later the pit of lions, because he stood up for The Lord in a pagan kingdom.

His three friends were thrown into a wilderness fire because they would not worship the king.

Jesus walked through the wilderness of temptation and came out in power on the other side.

Paul struggled continually in a wilderness of persecution, but advanced The Kingdom to the entire known world.

There is a way for you to walk through the wilderness of life. This way will cause you to step into your divine destiny and walk as a son no matter what the world may continue to throw at you. It may not be easy, but you will gain the power to set others free as you walk into the promise that awaits on the other side of the wilderness!

When viewed this way, the wilderness can be both attractive and repulsive at the same time. Only true warriors can make it through the wilderness. Practical experience and personal application of powerful principles have allowed me to walk The Wilderness Way. Here, there are no theories. Real, continuous struggle to overcome, and lessons learned, have helped me to understand how to walk into the promises for my life. **The Promised Land is on the other side of your wilderness.** May the powerful principles, and revelation of The Word applied in real life situations, help you to discover the pathway to promise that I have come to know as "The Wilderness Way!!!"

The Wilderness is calling, and I must go!!!

CHAPTER 1

THE WILDERNESS WAY

FROM AS LONG as I can remember, I have been drawn to Moses. His entire being characterized what God has been speaking and leading me into throughout my life. Many people focus on his divine birth: how he was saved, and his destination: where he ended up. However, **the majority of Moses' life was spent in the wilderness. This is where he was forged into the man of God we admire and desire to become.**

The first 40 years of his life, Moses was raised in opulence with every luxury known to man. Every comfort that he desired would have been quickly given to him without question. He had the finest wardrobe, tastiest food, most brilliant tutors, and greatest training in every area. He was never in lack or want for any imaginable thing. However, this was not the proper training ground to uncover his divine destiny. Continuously indulging in the pleasures of this life would only lead deeper and deeper into the bondage that plagues those who walk in the ways of the world.

Moses tried to put the lessons he had learned as an Egyptian into practice when he handled the situation with the taskmaster and Hebrew slave (*Exodus 2:11-15*). The yoke of bondage that he was under caused him to choose to act in a way that would not only lead him into more bondage, but destroy the position of power that had taught him to act out of his own selfish motives. The bondage of pride and selfishness that had been stimulated and stroked by the ways of the world had taught him to walk into a deeper, more oppressive servitude than he had ever been in before. He had everything that people at this time and moment seek to gain, and it caused him to damage and destroy his entire life. Everything was gone in one selfish, prideful choice.

You may often read the Bible and view it as a bunch of fairy tales. The characters in these stories are not seen as real people who lived and made choices according to what they knew and thought was right.

Just like today, the choices you make are often determined by the environment, pressures, and expectation that has surrounded you since birth. The world can only give you pain, suffering, and enslavement. Walking in bondage leads to deeper levels of enslavement. You may look at the lifestyle of others and desire to be like them never realizing they are actually living in a prison. Often, you may overlook the oppression and darkness all around and crave the very yoke that will bring death and destruction into your own life. You may get what you desire, but all the entrapments that you did not see at the time now have overtaken and left you hurting and vulnerable to even more torment.

This is what happened to Moses. He acted the way he was trained to and it caused pain, suffering, and destruction of everything, including his luxurious lifestyle. After that fateful decision, everything changed for Moses. All the wealth was stripped away, and he was left with nothing.

The next forty years of Moses' life was spent as a shepherd in the wilderness. He could never return to his old way of life because of the result of one fateful decision. He was a murderer, hiding on the back side of the desert, working in the most inconspicuous position he could find.

What happened in this place of testing, trying, hardship, and loneliness?

What wilderness lessons were being taught and worldly ways unlearned?

Moses had to come face to face with his pride and selfishness over and over again. No longer did he sleep on the softest beds with nice pillows and blankets of the finest quality. He began to become familiar with rocks, bugs, and the hard ground.

How many times did he think back to the palatial period and the comforts of that time?

His royalty had been stripped away, and now he was ruler over the lowly livestock in the middle of the wilderness. **It is here where he begins to unlearn the selfish, prideful, fleshly mentality.** Moses was no longer the highest class ruler. The smallest sheep took precedence over him now. Every calf, lamb, or kid must be cared for, protected, and valued far above his own comfort and safety.

For forty years, Moses unlearned everything that Egypt had taught him. The Hebrew word for Egypt is *"Mizraim"* which means double bondage. The people of God were enslaved not only in their body, but in their mind as well. **Moses, being born into the royal family, was not under physical chains, but his mind was imprisoned and yoked to the mentality of sin that leads to destruction and death.** Even though he had everything he could have ever wanted, he was enslaved by Egypt.

For Moses to be the deliverer God had destined him to become, he must be reshaped, remade, and reforged. The transformation that took place those forty years in the wilderness caused him to lose his pride and selfishness. After all the long years, he was finally bare and exposed. He was ready for an encounter with The Truth, his Creator.

Many people believe that the troubles and trials of this life are designed to take them out. This may be the case for those trying to fulfill their own plans and purposes, but when you find "The Wilderness Way," you will not only be able to survive the attacks but **the wilderness will become a forge for you to be transformed.**

A forge was a tool used to heat an object, usually metal, until it became red-hot and easily pliable to be purified, shaped, and sharpened. The blacksmith would use tongs and transfer the red hot piece of metal to an anvil. Using a hammer, he would begin to beat and shape it into a useful instrument. If the hammer and anvil were used without the forge and the fire, the tool would shatter and break.

God's plan is never for you to shatter and break. However, **you are not now what you are supposed to become.** God has a divine destiny over your life that has been purposed since the beginning of time. His plans and purposes are greater and better than you could possibly imagine. Compared to what He has for you, your thinking is so small that you would be astounded by all He has ordained for you to accomplish.

From the moment you are born into the world, you begin to be shaped and come into line with your family, environment, and relationships. Often, too late in life, you realize that others are trying to remake you in their own image. **It takes true revelation from God for you to see who you were created to be.** When this happens, you have a choice. *Do you submit to becoming who the Divine Designer has created you to be, or do you yield to your own intentions and desires?*

The selfish nature and the world beckon you to take the easy road. Do not change, do not conform to anything. At the same time, they will be reshaping you into the "non-conforming" image that they want you to be. The people of this world want to live in their own ways and for no one to judge them or make them change. The longer you walk around with this mentality, the deeper into the depths of darkness you will delve. The chains of imprisonment are being heaped upon you and there is no way to escape, other than through divine assistance.

A divine interruption to what is "natural" provides a way of escape. **The path out of darkness, and destruction is not attractive to the flesh. God offers you the forge.** The forge is uncomfortable and unyielding. As the heat is turned up, flesh, pride, and self slowly begin to melt away. Like fat, the useless parts began to sizzle and burn. Excess waste is destroyed. Before long, it seems like nothing is left of what you knew of yourself. This is the best place to be.

The world can never tell you who you really are. Your family, friends, school, or workplace do not actually know what you were made for. The Creator of the Universe who holds your divine destiny in His hands, the one who bled and died to give you freedom, life, and hope for eternity, is the only One able to reveal this. He is the One who dwells in Fire. He is completely pure and holy. He is the All-Consuming Fire!!!

As you come closer to the Fire, the things of this life are burned away. The forge is designed to burn away the junk and purify you not only to complete the plans and purposes that He has designed for you to accomplish, but for you to come closer to Him than ever before. Going through the forge leads to the fire!!!

It took forty years in the wilderness for Moses to be stripped, separated from Egypt, and prepared to meet The Lord. It was at this time that he saw the burning bush. Interestingly, God revealed himself in a picture like a forge. The burning bush, as it is called, was not burning at all. A fire that did not consume this bush on a mountain was truly a sight to see. The laws of nature were broken to reveal a unique part of the nature of God.

If the bush was not destroyed in the fire, would Moses be consumed in the fire?

God does not desire to consume or destroy you. He desires to purify you and make you holy that you may come close and become one with Him. Moses turned aside from himself to come close and see this oddity.

Moses had finally come to a point in walking in the wilderness that his ears were open to what God was speaking to him. Moses saw a manifestation of God and did not recognize it at first. He had never seen this before.

Why? He was too full of himself and the ways of Egypt.

Now that he has emptied himself, he is able to see God. As he draws near, he is able to hear God speaking clearly. The first thing that God begins to speak after He reveals Himself to Moses is divine destiny. He begins to call Moses to join Him in His work. God does not tell Moses to go and do something for Him. Instead, He reveals the plans and purposes that are in His heart. God then invites Moses to join this divine destiny.

In one moment, Moses sees, hears, and receives revelation that will change everything for him. The eyes of Moses have been circumcised from the Egyptian system. His ears have been purified and been made to hear the unseen secrets of his Creator. At this moment, Moses' heart is open, raw, and moldable to The Divine Blacksmith.

Even as the profound proclamation comes forth, Moses has the choice whether to embrace the awkward and uncomfortable calling or continue in his regular routine of living in the wilderness. **He is being called to go higher and deeper into his divine destiny by The One who spoke creation into existence.** However, it seems Moses is not quite ready for such a drastic change.

The invitation to step into the divine design is partnered with a new revelation of Moses' identity. God is bringing Moses back to Moses' original design that he had tried to fulfill in his own way and failed miserably. **He was always called to be a deliverer, however, he could never carry this out in his flesh.** To accept the call of the Lord, he must accept the identity that he had left behind.

What was Moses' response to this oracle of his eternal identity?

> *"But Moses said to God, 'Who am I, that I should go to Pharaoh, and that I should bring the children of Israel out of Egypt?'"*
> *Exodus 3:11*

Moses' identity was in question. The pride of being raised in Pharaoh's palace is now gone. He has accepted his life as a shepherd, and become comfortable in this calling. It is in this moment, The Spirit is calling him higher and deeper.

Interestingly, the word for wilderness and desert in Hebrew is the same. It comes from the root רבד (dabar) which means, "word". The literal Hebrew definition of wilderness is "the place of wording".[1]

The wilderness is the place of naming. All the formal ways of the world are abandoned. The place of naming is a place where true identity can be spoken into you by The One who created you. Here, you must come face to face with yourself. You begin to differentiate what others have said about you and what you have said about yourself. **As the voices are stripped away, you are able to seek The Lord and clearly hear what He says about you.** His calling is greater and higher than you could ever imagine. **Divine destiny and original design is eternally at war with the comforts of flesh and the Egyptian worldly system.** This becomes more evident the more God reveals His plans, purpose, and promise to you.

I had a dream several years ago that illustrates this point. In the dream, I was in a large gym that was crowded with all the people I knew or met throughout my lifetime. As happens in gyms, the conversations were amplified and becoming louder and more rowdy as the dream went on. I was looking among the masses trying to find my wife. Someone I knew was from Jesus (maybe an angel), was behind me trying to tell me where she was. After becoming so overwhelmed with the volume of voices, I shouted rather loudly, "Be quiet!" As all the voices became immediately silent, I noticed my wife in front of me a little to my left. She had been there the whole time, but I could not see or hear the voice of the Lord because of the noise.

All the voices around you will try to tell you who you are. They will speak what they see or mold you into their own image of you. This is how the worldly system works. However, **when God speaks your identity, it is not to mold you into His image, it is a revelation of who you are and who you were created to be.** He is not molding you as much as stripping away the things that are not you which have become attached to you. He helps you to discover your true self.

A true encounter with The Lord will begin freeing you from the bondage of the world and raise you up to begin walking into your heavenly calling. This can be confusing and overwhelming since you have been raised and trained in a structure that causes this to seem upside down. No longer is bias, opinion, and self-serving designation being thrust upon you, but righteous revelation of who you are for real. As uncomfortable as it may be to see and progress toward your God-given identity, it is necessary for you to advance in The Kingdom of God.

Still uncertain about the identity that is being revealed, Moses continues to question the directive that is being given to him.

> *"Then Moses said to God, 'Behold, when I come to the Israelites and say to them, 'The God of your fathers (ancestors) has sent me to you,' and they say to me, 'What is His name?' What shall I say to them?'"*
> *Exodus 3:13*

As God brings revelation of the core of your identity, He will bring insight into the unique message and voice that you have been given. The creation of your being was for a plan and purpose that only you can accomplish as you walk in The Wilderness Way.

Fear and insecurity will cause you to be silent and not speak out the message that God has given you. For example, when I was about nine years old, I was a very rambunctious child. My brother and I were always getting in trouble and were often justly punished for our mischief. However, one of these times, I felt like I needed to explain myself and was not given the chance. The enemy used this as an opportunity to speak a lie to me that plagued me for years afterward. This was the same lie that I believe he was speaking to Moses, and maybe even has spoken to you. This is the lie, "whatever I have to say does not matter."

The enemy played on my fear and insecurity with this lie to keep me silent in nearly every situation. God has called me with a gift of wisdom and speaking The Truth, and the enemy tried to shut this down by making me feel like I had nothing to say. Do not ever believe this lie. **Holy Spirit has given you a voice and a message that only you can speak.** No one else can declare what you have or express it from your unique perspective. You have a key no one else has, that others need, to unlock the chains of the burdens they have been struggling under for so long.

Fear and insecurity will cause you to bring up all kinds of excuses and rationalizations why you are disqualified from fulfilling the word God is speaking over you. These will be stripped away as you come closer to the forge in the wilderness.

The next excuse that Moses brings to the Lord is this:

> *"Then Moses answered [the Lord] and said, 'What if they will not believe me or take seriously what I say? For they may say, 'The Lord has not appeared to you.'"*
> *Exodus 4:1*

The message and voice that Moses has been given might not be effective in his own mind. Even if the words are valid and true, *what if it does not affect a change in the people who hear it?* The results may not live up to the expectations that Moses had set.

Here, the fear of the reception of the message and the belief of the authority is questioned. There will always be skeptics, doubters, and naysayers. However, you cannot let these, no matter how many or how few, keep you from speaking the Truth that will set the hungry and receptive people free from bondage. The results are in the hands of The Lord. If one person is set free by your ability to speak and proclaim The Word of The Lord, you are bearing fruit. **If you speak what God has given you in obedience to Him, especially in the face of fear, you are effective.**

God speaks to this fear and says again, *"I will be with you and prove the words from My mouth that you speak."* If Moses obeys and speaks, God will back up his words with signs and wonders because he will be speaking the words of The Lord Himself.

Whether Moses had begun to believe a lie or is trying to get out of the calling of The Lord, he brings up another reason why he thinks he cannot be used.

> *"Then Moses said to the Lord, 'Please, Lord, I am not a man of words (eloquent, fluent), neither before nor since You have spoken to Your servant; for I am slow of speech and tongue.'"*
> **Exodus 4:10**

Some scholars speculate that Moses has a speech impediment, but the New Testament states clearly that during his forty years in Egypt, Moses was *"...mighty in words and deeds"* (**Acts 7:22**). Forty years of being in the wilderness, with only a few people around, has convinced Moses that he is nobody, no one will listen to him, he has nothing to say, and cannot speak well. He has literally gone from one of the highest places in the society of that time to one of the lowest. It is here that God is able to meet with Moses and reveal the plans and purposes designed for him. Even after everything God speaks and reveals, Moses still struggles with stepping into the dynamic destiny that God Himself is declaring over him with multiple miraculous manifestations to his eyes and ears.

> *"But he said, 'Please my Lord, send the message [of rescue to Israel] by [someone else,] whomever else You will [choose].'"* **Exodus 4:13**

This is the final lie that has to be overcome. Surely someone else can carry the weight of this divine mandate on my life. God could choose anyone else, *why you?* **After The Word has been spoken, you must choose to listen, obey, and begin to step into *all* God has spoken over your life.** Stepping out in obedience will actually cause you to begin walking in The Wilderness Way.

Fire reproduces fire. When the manifestation of The Lord is revealed to you, His flames will purify you and burn up everything that is unnecessary. Moses could have chosen to venture back out into the wilderness again, but this is not where he, or you, are called to live. Everyone will walk in the wilderness and the fleshly things will be challenged, but for the few that choose to walk in The Way in the wilderness, they will encounter The True and Living God again and again as He refines, purifies and reveals His presence over and over.

Once you encounter the fire, you are never the same. You will always long for more and deeper. **The wilderness will change you for the better or it will make you bitter.** Everyone will walk through the wilderness and have an encounter with fire. They may see but never experience and step into The Truth. Some may come close and get burned then return to their old ways. However, the few that see, hear, and come close to the fire will never be the same (*Isaiah 43:1-2*).

Do you want to become better or bitter?

The forge is not pleasant, but The Presence leading you through will not allow you to be harmed. He will reveal the real you. The Wilderness is not meant to destroy but to sharpen and hone your edge to become the mighty weapon of war (*Jeremiah 51:20*) you were designed to be.

The Wilderness Way is designed to bring freedom to your life. This worldly system has placed bondage and chains upon you. Strongholds of sin have been built up in your life to keep you from fulfilling your divine mandate. God is The One who is calling you out into the wilderness. **When you look to Him, He will lead you through the wilderness, through the fire, through the valley of the shadow of death.** He is walking with you and leading you into freedom.

Freedom reproduces freedom. As you are led by The Spirit in The Wilderness Way, you are gaining freedom and life that you could not receive any other way. One of the first things that will be implanted in you is the desire to bring others to this place of freedom as well.

Moses had one encounter with The Lord at The Fire, and he was never the same. Even though he resisted in the flesh everything God was calling him to do, his spirit recognized who he was called to be and bore witness with what was spoken. **From this point, Moses began to walk in the way that would lead not only himself into a deeper level of freedom and life, but all those who would follow him.** He was transformed by the power of The Word and given a mandate to do the same for his people. **This is your directive as well. Walk in The Wilderness Way and call others out of their bondage to encounter the Fire of The Spirit of Truth for themselves.**

"So He said, 'I will certainly be with you. And this shall be a sign to you that I have sent you: When you have brought the people out of Egypt, you shall serve God on this mountain.'"
Exodus 3:12

In my own life, I have come to several times of decision. About the age of sixteen, one of these choices was placed before me. I had been training for about eight years in Judo. Much like wrestling, this is a martial art I enjoyed and excelled in. So much so, I traveled to Arizona to compete in the junior Olympics. At the same time, God was calling and drawing me deeper into him. In the eyes of the world, I could literally become famous because of my physical accomplishments, or I could follow the leading of The King.

I remember that I made a conscious shift both in the physical and spiritual to begin to pursue the things of The Lord over these physical things. The desire to continue martial arts did not diminish, but God was beginning to reveal my true self. I would not be changed staying in the worldly system. **Pursuing The Lord and all He had for me would start me on the path that would lead me to where I am now.** The change was not easy and did not make sense to those around me, but looking back, this has helped me to step up into a new calling and divine purpose of wrestling in the spirit.

I pray that as you come to your time of decision that you are not paralyzed in fear or indecision but yield completely to the forge and begin to walk fully into the Divine destiny revealed upon The Wilderness Way.

CHAPTER 2

THE VISION

IN CHAPTER ONE, we talked about the transformation that took place in Moses after he went out into the wilderness. Here, he was stripped of the bondage, ways of the world, and was able to encounter The Lord as he never had before. During the encounter at the burning bush, God brings insight to Moses' true identity, mission, calling and how he is to accomplish it. Even though Moses resists at first, eventually, he complies with The Spirit of God, and takes steps of obedience.

We are called to lead people out of bondage to the place of encounter by advancing the Truth!

I walked in so much bondage as a young person even though I was raised in a godly family with amazing Spirit-filled parents. We gathered at the table together, went to church together, ministered together, and still I became entangled in the affairs of this life. It is not hard for me to imagine those who have no support system, or who are first-generation Christians, have so much from which to get free.

The good news is that when we come to Christ, He *"raises us all up to be seated together in heavenly places with Him"* (*Ephesians 2:6*).

Moses is called out of Egypt so that he could become free from the

Egyptian system in mind and body. He had to become completely cut off and free from everything for a period of forty years that he could encounter The Truth through the fiery bush on the mountain.

From the bush, God speaks clearly that He has come to set His people free from Egypt. Affliction, pain, and suffering is all that they will gain living in the worldly system. Moses understood this because even though he had been spoiled in luxury, he experienced the same bondage in his soul which led to the actions that brought about his exile.

As was mentioned before, Egypt means double bondage. Freedom reproduces freedom, but bondage begets more bondage. The people had lived for generations in oppression, and their mindset had become accustomed to their new way of life. The chains of their bodies had begun to change their minds. Such strongholds had been built up in them that even after they were free in their bodies, they wanted to return over and over into slavery. It was easier to live as a slave than to walk into freedom in the wilderness living by faith, and patiently persisting in waiting on the promises of God -this was completely out of the question!

The Egyptian mindset was such a stronghold that many never got free. An entire generation, except for two individuals, chose bondage and death over The Promised Land. They were led through the wilderness for forty years being given every opportunity to encounter God on The Mountain. In fact, these are the same people that once heard the thunderous voice of The Lord and never wanted to hear it again. They did not want to turn aside and come close, but they wanted a ruler to tell them what to do so they could stay at a comfortable distance holding onto their chains. These all died in the wilderness. They were not changed so they kept their chains.

The people were still slaves to Egypt because they were not able to be freed from the identity of a slave and become the sons and daughters that God was calling them to be. God called them to riches and royalty with Him, but they were too accustomed to their life of lack and being continually stolen from.

Moses encountered the Lord and was given this new identity. Although it was difficult for him to accept, he was willing to take a step in the right direction. He came close to the bush and took off his sandals at the word of The Lord. This was the first step in the right direction. **This first act of obedience opened Moses up to receive revelation of his identity, purpose, and power.** These things are only found in God, and cannot be fully uncovered or unlocked any other way.

Moses's time in the wilderness taught him not to trust himself; he acquired humility (pride was stripped from him). **You must be stripped of the rags of slavery that you may receive the righteous robes of a ruler.**

One encounter with God revealed Moses' true God-given identity and purpose. He was empowered and enabled to complete the next step of this process by trust and obedience in the prophetic words spoken to him during this encounter.

Moses' calling can be summed up in one verse:

> *And God said, "Certainly I will be with you, and this shall be the sign to you that it is I who have sent you: when you have brought the people out of Egypt, you shall serve and worship God at this mountain."*
> **Exodus 3:12**

God will be with Moses. **The power of God comes from His presence.** Moses comes to truly understand and contends for this later when He declares that he will not go anywhere unless God goes with them.

God has sent him. Since God is not only with Moses but has sent him, Moses' way has been prepared. There is a way, for Moses to walk in, where the blessing of life and power resides.

The Spirit says clearly *"when"* you have brought the people out of Egypt not *"if"*. This is the promise that he will be successful.

Moses is called to bring the people out of bondage. For someone who tried to do this in his own power and failed miserably, this would be extremely intimidating.

Moses is called to lead the newly freed people to the same place he had encountered The Lord. God desires to meet with them in the same way He is encountering Moses. **God desires to encounter you personally in the same way. He is calling you out of the strongholds that have been built up in your life to a true encounter with Him.** He is ready to speak to you if you will turn aside from the worldly system and come near to Him.

If you study what takes place on The Mountain of God, the people are given boundaries to stay away during three days of purification. While here, they see the lightning and fire on The Mountain. They smell the smoke, maybe even tasting it in the air. They hear a trumpet blast and thunderings. There is no doubt in anyone's mind that God is on this mountain. God actually speaks to all the people with His mighty voice, and they do not want to hear it.

What would cause you to reject The Word of The Lord when He speaks and shows Himself to you?

Only a true encounter with your Creator can reveal your God-given identity and set you completely free. Here is the problem. We have been living in bondage for so long that we have become comfortable in it and enslaved in our minds. Freedom and responsibility actually becomes scary to us. Fear of the unknown overwhelms and keeps us willingly in torment. But, we think we know who we are because the world tells us. Although we desire to be unique, we become like all the others that are told what to do, say, and think.

When they rejected The Word of The Lord and His invitation to an encounter on The Mountain, the people had already lost The Promised Land. The physical location was nothing compared to the transcendent presence of The Lord. They were invited to ascend to a level of atmospheric acceleration, but they could not untangle themselves from the fetters that kept them in subjugation. Before they saw the giants and their fortresses, they had already given away the power and identity that was being handed to them.

From this point, they were choosing a wilderness life only. The wilderness is not bad when you will learn from it -when The Lord leads you into and through The Wilderness Way. **The trials and temptations will lead to triumph if you grow to a place of encountering and overcoming your own weakness.** There is a way in the wilderness that leads to The Mountain of Encounter. This is where The Spirit of God speaks identity, frees you from bondage, and causes you to overcome. You will never walk The Wilderness Way on your own unless you choose to accept the help that is offered to you. Instead, you choose a life of wandering aimlessly in the wilderness.

The first place to encounter God was walking through the wilderness to The Mountain. Often, during the testing times, your mindset can become clouded, and you do not realize that Holy Spirit is using these times to purge and purify. **The wilderness strips you of the ways of the world, pride, rebellion, and unbelief if you walk in humility and perseverance.** Freedom comes through persistent purification if you are willing to go through the fire and walk in The Way. The Spirit wants to lead you out of the wilderness to The Mountain, but you have to walk with Him in faith, obedience, and perseverance which is contrary to your own comfortable, selfish heart. You are being drawn to The Mountain if you will walk with The Spirit in The Wilderness Way.

The Mountain is the place where God dwells. Holiness is necessary to press into the deepest places with Him. This is where your true God-given identity and purpose is revealed. This is where you are empowered to walk in the new places He is calling you. This is where new abilities, gifts, and connections are made to enable you to advance into new levels in The Kingdom.

Isaiah 35 speaks of a transformation in the wilderness of those who follow The Spirit of God. The Wilderness Way is not a desolate, abandoned, or weary path if you are living and walking by The Spirit. Gladness, joy, exaltation, and fruitfulness are found in the wilderness when you embrace the beauty of what is taking place. The glory, majesty, and splendor of God is revealed in the desert place if you are with The Lord.

There are many traveling through this place that are exhausted, weak, and full of fear. In this desolate place there are ones who are blind, deaf, lame, and mute because of the ways they have been ensnared and given over to the enemy. **Any area that you agree with the enemy, you give him your power to see, hear, speak, and even walk.** In giving up these things, you become useless in The Kingdom of God unless you can somehow gain your freedom.

I desire to encourage and strengthen you. The salvation and deliverance of The Lord is at hand. He is with you right where you are. **What looked like a desolate wasteland can become a fruitful field if you yield to Him.** You can receive daily provision and manna right where you are. Water will come forth from the very rocks in the desert if you are open to The Spirit.

There is a Wilderness Way that leads to The Mountain of Encounter. This is where you are called to walk. Do not live your life continually walking around in circles struggling to survive. Continue seeking The Lord through the confusion, and you will come to the straight and narrow path. This will lead to The Mountain where you will encounter The Truth in a way you never have before. Your identity, destiny, and purpose will be revealed, and you will be increasingly liberated as you walk in faith, obedience, and perseverance.

This is what you are called to! This is who you are!

You are not of the world that draws back in fear to destruction, but you are one of us who believes to the salvation, healing, and deliverance of the soul (paraphrase of *Hebrews 10:39*).

CHAPTER 3

RAISING HUNGRY HEARTS

S OMEONE CANNOT GO from total bondage to complete freedom
in one easy step. We are so entangled in the system of the world
that the normal progression to uninhibited life takes continual obedience and faith to move forward.

**The first step on the journey toward change is hunger. Everything
starts with Hunger!**

The place where you are now does not have to be where you remain.
The Israelites in captivity were unhappy with their way of life. This is
when they began to cry out to God. They wanted change. Later when
they were in the forge being purified, they would cry out to return to
the chains because they had become so comfortable with them.

Jesus directly addresses hunger early on in His ministry.

> *"On the last day, that great day of the feast, Jesus stood and cried
> out, saying, 'If anyone thirsts, let him come to Me and drink.'"*
> *John 7:37*

Here, Jesus is not addressing a physical desire. Notice, this is the last
day of a feast. People would have completely satiated their physical de-

sire for food and drink. Much like Thanksgiving afternoon when many are lounging on the couch watching football. No one really wants to talk about the amount of food they have just consumed or the abundance of leftovers that are left to gorge themselves on later.

Jesus is addressing a desire in the spirit for freedom, change, and something different. When you are in bondage, you get caught in a continuous routine of bondage and action that leads to deeper bondage. This is the downward spiral that you may easily see in others, but rarely in yourself.

There is a spiritual desire within every single person to know who they are and to do what they are designed to do. The meaning of life is a question that has been contemplated since the beginning of time, but cannot be answered apart from The One from whom all life flows.

You will come to a point in your life of complete desperation for something different. This will not be the same for every individual, but **when you realize that you cannot live and become free in your own power, you will be determined to do something different. This is when you become hungry.**

Hunger will cause you to do things you normally would not do.

Moses was to lead the people to The Mountain and show them how they could encounter God. **Their hunger and desire to be free would cause them to do whatever it would take to encounter God for themselves.** In the midst of the crowds of people that were led out of bondage, there were a few hungry people that would adamantly refuse to return to Egypt. These clung desperately onto The Word being spoken by Moses and by God from The Mountain. They heard and caught something that was not able to be received by everyone else. Their ears had been freed just enough to receive the revelation, and they chose to walk into freedom no matter what it would cost them.

What you hunger for is what you will begin to look like!!! Those who continually give in to the pleasures of their palate, fat-filled foods, and lethargy, like the proverbial couch potato, will begin to look like a fat-filled potato themselves. Those who idolized a certain movie star or sports figure will begin to dress and act like them. It is easy to see how this plays out in the physical, but *what does your spiritual appetite say about you?*

You must hunger for The Holy One and become holy just the same. As you hunger for the only One who can truly satisfy, you can be sure of this:

> *"He is a rewarder of those who diligently seek Him"*
> **Hebrews 11:6**

God does not tease you with a taste of something you cannot have. It gives Him joy to increasingly reward each and every act of obedience with more of Who He is. This is true from the New to the Old Testament. If you follow The Holy One walking in His way, He will lead you into increasing levels of freedom and purification so that you can come closer to Him than ever before.

> *"'And you will seek Me and find Me, when you search for Me with all your heart. I will be found by you,' says the Lord, 'and I will bring you back from your captivity...'"*
> **Jeremiah 29:13-14**

Here, the prophet is speaking of God bringing the people back from physical captivity, but spiritual captivity precedes physical captivity. The enemy will overtake your spirit, heart, and mind first then you will become his physical prisoner. The path to freedom will come as you get free in the spirit then you will be able to walk into complete and total freedom.

Another promise from God that conveys His heart to satisfy the hungry is:

> *"Blessed are those who hunger and thirst after righteousness, for they shall be filled."*
> **Matthew 5:6** (NKJV)

Jesus is teaching His disciples during the Sermon on the Mount and disclosing the heart, attitude, and actions that unlock the blessings of Heaven. Attention is drawn once again to this attitude of hunger for a right relationship with God. When you are hungry and truly desire something, you will never let anything get in your way. You will do whatever it takes to lay hold of the treasure that has captured your gaze. Desiring righteousness, or a right relationship with God, is guaranteed to fill you up but not to satisfy your hunger. **In The Kingdom of God, the more you hunger and receive, the hungrier you will become.** Continual hunger leads to continual filling with more.

David repeatedly shares this desire for a deeper relationship with The Lord. The greater he came to know a small part of the mysteries of The Mighty One, the more he desired. Here are a couple of places he describes how much he wants more:

> *"As the deer pants for the water brooks, So pants my soul for You, O God. My soul thirsts for God, for the living God..."*
> **Psalm 42:1-2**

> *"... My soul thirsts for You; My flesh longs for You In a dry and thirsty land Where there is no water. So I have looked for You..."*
> **Psalm 63:1-2**

A right and true desire to draw near to God and delve deeper into the infinity of knowing Him can only be explained in the natural by a hunger or thirst. However, the incessant gnawing of the soul for a union with its creator is an insatiable craving that is unexplainable by natural means.

Hunger, in the natural, points to a greater need for something outside yourself. While walking through the darkness of the world, you can snack on the tasty treats that are laid before you, but they turn sour in your stomach. There is no long-lasting benefit from satiating your appetite with these trifles. *What am I speaking of here?* Endless hours of Netflix and media entertainment, sleep, food of every kind, style, status, and all the things money can buy. These are not necessarily wrong, but neither are they beneficial for building The Kingdom.

It is true that God *"satisfies your mouth with good things..."* (**Psalm 103:5**), but this should not be your ambition to acquire. The appetite and love for these things will influence you to travel on a path that will rapidly lead to sin and death. Instead, when you follow after God, He will satisfy you with good and profitable things that build up The Kingdom.

All throughout The Word, God urges you to walk on the path of righteousness that leads to life. He directs you to choose life in every circumstance. **You have a choice to walk in your own way or walk in the righteous pathway.** There is only one safe passage through the storms, trials, and wilderness that everyone must go through. You must walk this way to be forged and refined so that you may become a seed that bears fruit and reproduces abundant life for The Kingdom.

The river of life flows from the throne of God, and contains an astounding promise:

> *"I will pour water on him who is thirsty and floods on the dry ground..."*
> **Isaiah 44:3**

So you do not think that this happens because of who you are or what you have done, God reveals that this is because He has created you, and He has chosen you. **It is your divine inheritance to receive the life and blessing that flows from Heaven, and these things are continually available to you.** However, you do not receive these things by being alive or by chance. The blessings of The Lord come in fullness when you seek Him. When you come into the presence of The Lord and begin to truly know Him, you will desire to pursue Him in a deeper way. As you have a greater desire for The Lord, He will pour out increasingly more upon you.

The invitation to come and drink is not only for those who know The Lord, but for anyone and everyone who is thirsty.

"Ho! Everyone who thirsts, come to the waters..."
Isaiah 55:1

No one is excluded from the water of life. However, you will disqualify yourself if you are satiating your desires with the things of the world. You will not hunger or thirst for true life if you are filled up with the trifling morsels that are offered by the dealers of death.

Your desire for something different will cause you to move from where you are, just as the Hebrews were compelled to leave Egypt. Sometimes, you may become accustomed to the repetitive rut that has been carved out from the shadows of death and the gloom of those who are doomed. The enemy of our souls desires to entomb all who trudge through the mire of mediocrity. Deep inside, there is a cry of the heart for deeper meaning and purpose. Your spirit knows that you were created for more than a meaningless existence following in the fads and footsteps of others. It is from this place that a groaning and cry for the greater will draw you to the never-ending river of life that is free for all those who will come.

"I will give of the fountain of the water of life freely to him who thirsts."
Revelation 21:6

This life sustaining force is forever flowing freely because of the priceless sacrifice of your eternal Savior. The greater your desire is, the more you are able to receive.

Jesus is the Reward of those who hunger and thirst after Him. From the beginning, a secret is revealed to Abram that is the same oracle to you today.

"...I am your shield, your exceedingly great reward."
Genesis 15:1

The reward of desire for the Lord is more revelation of Him. The result of knowing Him is a deeper hunger and thirst to come into union with this mystery made known. **The reward for the hungry is Jesus and more hunger!**

In 2012, I traveled to London to be a part of an outreach surrounding the Summer Olympics that were being held in that location. While there ministering with crazy evangelists, one of my friends, Sage, invited me to join him on a scouting trip to India. Honestly, I did not want to go for a myriad of reasons. However, I truly desired to do the will of The Lord and what He had for me. After a time of focused fasting, prayer, and laying down of my flesh, I knew that I was supposed to join Sage on this trip.

Later on, as I was out in the local town looking for where to join The Lord in His work, I heard the Lord say to me "I did not call you to England just to do this outreach. If you had not said yes to come to England you never would have gone to India." I wanted to argue within myself that I would have been obedient no matter where I was, but *who can argue with God?*

India became my delight. I chose to serve the Lord no matter how my flesh might not like it. It is my delight to do God's will. The next few weeks of trying to get where I was supposed to go in India was almost comical. I waited for a visa, flew to the wrong place in India, could not contact the people I was going to be staying with and more. It took three full days to get to the middle of nowhere India, a place I had never been, to stay with people I had never met, and I still arrived before Sage.

If I had not been hungry to do the will of The Lord, any one of the number of setbacks I encountered could have been an excuse to turn back. I ended up staying in India for about a month traveling and ministering in different places. The relationships I made while there opened the door for me to come back and minister the following year with my wife. India became one of our most favorite places. Although the living conditions were markedly different than that of The States, the people were ravenous for The Lord. This allowed God to move in amazing supernatural ways that we had not seen in other places.

My desire to do the will of The Lord opened the door for more to be done and revealed to me and through me more than I thought possible. It created within me a new hunger to see these same things take place wherever I went. **Hunger for The Lord and obedience to His word created more hunger and drew me closer than ever before.** I chose to move into what was uncomfortable and completely different than what I had ever known before. *Why?* I did this because I was hungry. I encountered The Lord on The Mountain and determined never to shrink back but to press in and receive the fullness of the promise. I purposed that the former things (Egypt) would no longer have a hold on me because I desired all that God had promised no matter what I had to leave behind.

Increasing hunger and depth in knowing Jesus the great and limitless reward will lead you to His Holy Fire. **Hungry people will be drawn to The Fire!**

CHAPTER 4

TRAINING BURNING ONES

A LL OVER THE world, in every area of society and culture, there is a group of people that is hidden, waiting, seeking. Some have referred to these as, "the remnant". They are the hungry hearts ready to make a change. They see the systems and what the normal progression of life will cause them to become, but they disagree. This is not for them. **The expectations of the world are not the ways of The Kingdom.** The remnant are those who are history makers. They walk differently and live in a manner inconsistent with the world. Masses of people desire to be unique, but few will do the work necessary to get to that place. Jesus said it this way:

> *"For many are called, but few are chosen."*
> **Matthew 22:14**

The call to come up to the next level is hanging like a low-lying fruit in the atmosphere ready to be picked. But only some will choose to take it. Fewer still will take and eat it. And those who will begin to reproduce what is found in the fruit seem to be fewer still. Anyone can take the fruit; however, only the hungry will fully consume that which God has for them.

I grew up in an amazing family. Our family life was centered around

The Lord. My father made a choice that he would raise his family in the gospel. I do not even know what kind of sacrifice this must have been for him. We, his children, reaped the benefits.

As a child, I always went to Sunday School and church, memorized Bible verses and the like. Many people were constantly coming into our home to be discipled, trained, and to seek the Lord together. Throughout all this, I learned the importance of the gospel, but never fully stepped in. I desired to please The Lord and walk in His way. I felt a call to ministry from seventeen years old. I went to a Bible-based college and learned all the stuff, but I was only licking the outside of the fruit. As much as I wanted to walk in The Way, I was still overcome by the religious system of the world.

There were little glimmers throughout college, and afterwards, of those who were hungry that were pressing into something real. Now, I know I was searching for myself. I remember after I was placed into a leadership position at a church, Holy Spirit led me into the place of purging. As this purging took place, my hunger for The Lord changed me into an instrument of righteousness to be used by The Lord more and more as I placed myself in the fire.

Those who are hungry will be led to the fire. At this time, many will turn away from the intensity of the heat, but **those who are truly hungry will walk into the fire willingly, that they may be purified in the forge.**

After forty years, Moses had become accustomed to his way of life as a shepherd. He knew there was more and desired it, but did not know how to step into the next level. He was following the natural progression of the people he was with, his worldly culture. **He was caught in the monotony of daily life, but he was hungry.**

I believe that God led him to where he could see the fire off in the distance, but it was out of his way. Moses had to turn aside from his normal duties to come close to The Fire. In this abnormal, out of the way location, God speaks to Moses and tells him *"Do not come near..."* (*Exodus 3:5*).

Why did God say this?

I believe when Moses realized that God was there in the bush, he would have reached out and touched The Fire. However, it is easy to see that Moses still had in him fear, insecurity, and a desire to do things his own way. He was still in a spiritual bondage. Because of the hunger in his heart, Moses was able to come as close as possible, but God had to stop him before his impurity and unholiness caused him to be completely consumed in the presence of God.

As much as God loved His people and desired them to be free from their bondage, He cared for Moses and was empowering him to become free as well. The entire time Moses was leading the people, God was calling him to overcome fear of man and insecurity that had formerly bound him.

So, intentional was the refining of Moses that when he leads the people back to the mountain, he is able to go up on the mountain and see God in a way that no other man could. He was able to press into the fire on the mountain while everyone else drew back in fear. **Moses stepped into the fire because of the hunger in his heart to know The Lord.** At this point, Moses did not care if he died, he had to be as close to God as possible. He even desired to look upon the very face of God, which was forbidden. When he is told that no man can look upon God and live, he does not move from this place.

All throughout the Biblical account it is evident that for **those who are hungry, God comes as a fire.**

- Fire guards the way to the tree of life

> *"...He placed cherubim at the east of the garden of Eden, and a flaming sword which turned every way, to guard the way to the tree of life."*
> **Genesis 3:24** NKJV

Impurity and unrighteousness cannot gain access to The Tree of Life.

You must go through the fire to eat the fruit of abundant life that God has for you.

> *- Abraham enters into covenant with the Fire of God to follow and obey Him for generations*
>
> *"And it came to pass, when the sun went down and it was dark, that behold, there appeared a smoking oven and a burning torch that passed between those pieces."*
> **Genesis 15:17** NKJV

After Abraham was given the revelation that The Creator of the Universe is his great reward, God reveals Himself as a flaming torch to make a covenant with him. Not only is this an enduring covenant with an eternal God, it is one of continuing depths of holiness and coming close to The Flame.

> *- Moses and the people of God are lead by fire in the middle of the darkest night*
>
> *"And the Lord went before them by day in a pillar of cloud to lead the way, and by night in a pillar of fire to give them light, so as to go by day and night."*
> **Exodus 13:21** NKJV

In the middle of the darkest, coldest nights in the desert, God was a pillar of fire. For forty years God shows up every night as a fire. The people unaccustomed to and afraid of the fire stayed far away and were never changed to enter The Promised Land. The children that grew up with and played by the fire were transformed by it and inherited the promises.

> *- God speaks from The Fire on The Mountain*
>
> *"Then you came near and stood at the foot of the mountain, and the mountain burned with fire to the midst of heaven, with darkness,*

cloud, and thick darkness. And the Lord spoke to you out of the midst of the fire..."
Deuteronomy 4:11-12 NKJV

All the people heard the words of God coming from The Fire on the Mountain. None could deny that God was in the midst of this fire. **They trembled and moved away from The Fire even as they were invited to come near. This caused them to remain the same,** and they gave up the right to enter The Promised Land.

Who would dare to draw near the presence of The God who dwells in The Fire and speaks?

- Fire consumes Gideon's sacrificial offering

"Then the Angel of the Lord put out the end of the staff... and fire rose out of the rock and consumed the meat and the unleavened bread..."
Judges 6:21 NKJV

God desires to purify everything you will give Him. The things that are a waste will be consumed, but the eternal things will be purged, refined, and made new into an eternal sacrifice to a living God.

- Fire from heaven consumes Elijah's sacrifice. It is a sign for the people to turn their hearts back to God.

"...Elijah the prophet came near and said, "' Lord God of Abraham, Isaac, and Israel, let it be known this day that You are God in Israel... that this people may know that You are the Lord God, and that You have turned their hearts back to You again.'" Then the fire of the Lord fell and consumed the burnt sacrifice...Now when all the people saw it, they fell on their faces; and they said, "'The Lord, He is God! The Lord , He is God!'"
1 Kings 18:36-39 NKJV

It says that Elijah came near as he spoke these words.

How close was Elijah to the sacrifice?

Is it possible that The Fire came from heaven and completely consumed all the junk and rested on Elijah?

Everything was consumed in the fire of God but His prophet was consecrated to Him for the work of The Kingdom. **The Fire of God revealed what was pure, holy, and righteous and what needed to be consumed and destroyed.** The people realizing the Truth immediately proclaim the supremacy of God over all other things of this world.

- God rules from a throne of fire

"I watched till thrones were put in place, And the Ancient of Days was seated; His garment was white as snow, And the hair of His head was like pure wool. His throne was a fiery flame, Its wheels a burning fire; A fiery stream issued And came forth from before Him..."
Daniel 7:9-10 NKJV

God sits in the midst of fire. He rules from the fire. He moves with fire. He sends out fire before Him like a river. Righteousness, holiness, and justice surround Him. **If you desire to come close to Him, you must go through the fire of purification yourself.**

- Fire rested upon the disciples in the upper room

"And suddenly there came a sound from heaven, as of a rushing mighty wind, and it filled the whole house where they were sitting. Then there appeared to them divided tongues, as of fire, and one sat upon each of them. And they were all filled with the Holy Spirit and began to speak with other tongues, as the Spirit gave them utterance."
Acts 2:2-4 NKJV

Formerly, The Fire covenanted with man, rested upon the holy mountain of God, came and consumed the sacrifice, now it is resting upon those who are being obedient and seeking to draw near to Him. **It is filling completely the vessels that have made themselves ready and been made righteous by the blood of Jesus.** Never before had this been possible.

When the Fire of Holy Spirit comes, He comes to transform, purify, and change completely. The spiritual composition of a believer that continually places themselves in The Fire is radically different from the one who cannot come near.

- Followers of Jesus will be baptized with The Holy Spirit and Fire

*"I indeed baptize you with water unto repentance, but He who is coming after me... will baptize you with the Holy Spirit and fire... He will burn up the chaff with unquenchable fire." **Matthew 3:11-12** NKJV*

Followers of Jesus will place themselves continually in The Fire to be changed by it. They will do this so they can come close to the God who dwells in the fire.

Fire burns up all the useless junk that clings to you. So many things of this world try to weigh you down and hold you back. The fire is intense, but will cause all these things to be consumed and free you from the trappings and bondages of this life. **This intense fire is The Forge of The Lord that all those who hunger after Him must be transformed by.**

- The Word of God is revealed as a fire to the prophet Jeremiah

"'Is not My word like a fire?'" says the Lord, "'And like a hammer that breaks the rock in pieces?'"
Jeremiah 23:29

When God speaks, it rearranges the things in our lives. He breaks the bondages of this life and frees us to rise to new heights with Him. A hammer breaks and builds. A fire burns, purifies, and strengthens.

The Fire is The Word, power, and love embodied in Jesus. **You must become completely saturated with The Word (Jesus), with the love of The Father, and the power of Holy Spirit.**

> - *The very call of the prophet is to speak the fiery word of God and yield in obedience to these commands.*
>
> *"See, I have this day set you over the nations and over the kingdoms, To root out and to pull down, To destroy and to throw down, To build and to plant."*
> ***Jeremiah 1:10***

The rooting out, throwing down, and destroying is the old mindsets of the past and of the enemy that have set themselves up as false rulers to enslave not just people, but generations. Those who will not draw near the presence of God cannot get free of worldly systems. A revolution needs to take place, but this cannot happen outside of The Fiery Forge of refining and purifying. There are only two Kingdoms. To build one up you must tear down the other. The thoughts, that have been ingrained within you because of this world and the consequences that have come as you agreed with these things, must be destroyed in The Fire and replaced with the very words of God. This is how you will progressively advance into the divine destiny that you have been given. **Only by placing yourself continually in The Fire will you be forged and shaped into who you were made to be, A Burning One!**

> - *The Unshakeable Kingdom has been built in the midst of The Fire.*
>
> *"Therefore, since we are receiving a kingdom which cannot be shaken, let us have grace, by which we may serve God acceptably with reverence and godly fear. For our God is a consuming fire."*
> ***Hebrews 12:28-29*** NKJV

The commodities of this world cannot touch this eternal righteous Kingdom. God continually purifies all those who would desire to come close to His throne. Every pitiful and worthless system of the world or false ruler will be completely consumed in the righteousness and justice of The Lord. The waste will be wasted and the valuable will remain.

> *- The Burning Ones will always seek to place themselves in greater degrees of fire.*

The Fire of God is His Word, His power and His love, which comes through greater levels of holiness, consecration, and sacrifice. You cannot go to a deeper level unless you are willing to give up the lesser things. Even the writer of **Hebrews** speaks of this when he says, "*let us lay aside every weight and the sin that so easily ensnares us...*" (**12:1**).
The hungry are drawn to the refining, consuming fire, the forge. **You must be refined and made new to come closer. Those desiring to go deeper will do whatever it takes to get to the next level.** Nothing compares to the reward you will gain from The One who dwells in the fire as you come close to Him.

> *- Father, Son, and Holy Spirit are present in the forge.*

In the Old Testament, God the Father bases his judgment on actions. Abraham obeyed God. Lot did not. What these people did proved their obedience. When Jesus, The Word, came on the scene, he began to draw attention to the words that came from the people and the heart that was behind them. This was because The Holy Spirit was with Him. The words that came from Jesus were the words of God, and He brought attention to the importance of what you say, "*For by your words you will be justified, and by your words you will be condemned*" (**Matthew 12:37** NKJV).

> *- The Word of God judges the words that come out of you.*

The Holy Spirit was given to refine the thoughts and intents of the heart. He is with you to continually refine how you think which will lead to how you speak and act. The forge takes place at every area, and each aspect of the Trinity will be involved if you place yourself in the fire and become "a Burning One."

> *- The love of the Father is what will be used to judge your actions when you come into The Kingdom.*

This is stated in *Exodus*, "*but showing graciousness and steadfast lovingk-indness to thousands [of generations]...*" (**20:6**). The mercy of The Lord is great, but the actions are the result of the words spoken and thoughts allowed to take root. Judgment and mercy for actions comes from the loving Father who desires to correct and discipline in order for you to grow and be fruitful.

The Word is Jesus, and Jesus is The Word. Even when Jesus was tempted, He judged the words coming from the enemy. They sounded good but were just a little off. He is The Word and displays the heart of The Father lined up with the word of the mouth. Jesus spoke what He saw His Father doing. When the power of Holy Spirit comes upon the word, when the thoughts and intents of the heart line up with the word spoken, the actions produced will bring forth an abundant harvest. **This is what being a Burning One is all about, partnering with The Triune God, being IN His fire.**

- The power of Holy Spirit coming upon you and dwelling within you is to purify and refine your thoughts, desires, and intentions.

You can say the right thing and even have good actions like the Pharisees, but if your heart is not right you have missed it. Holy Spirit brings the power as you line up your heart with The Father. **Everything must flow from a purified heart to bring forth the best result.**
When the Spirit purifies the thoughts, Jesus refines the words, and the love of The Father demonstrates these God-given desires and precious

promises, the forge has crafted a mighty weapon to be used to advance The Kingdom of God, a Burning One!

- The more pure you become, the closer you can come to The Fire of God.

"And I will bring the third part through the fire, Refine them as silver is refined, And test them as gold is tested. They will call on My name, And I will listen and answer them; I will say, 'They are My people,' And they will say, 'The Lord is my God.'"
Zechariah 13:9

You are never meant to stay motionless in the fire. Like a piece of metal you must be rotated and shaped so you do not burn. You are to pass through the fire. He will bring you through it without being burned if you stay close to Him. You are not alone! **Total purity should be the goal so that you can be closer to Him than ever before.** The testing comes to prove the purity that has already taken place as you have passed through the fire.

As you come close, you know Him more. As you know God more, more of your identity is revealed, solidified, and strengthened. **You cannot become who you were created to be without passing through the fire!**

- Outward actions are only part of what God wants to purify.

"But who can endure the day of His coming? And who can stand when He appears? For He is like a refiner's fire and like launderer's soap [which removes impurities and uncleanness]. He will sit as a refiner and purifier of silver, and He will purify the sons of Levi [the priests], and refine them like gold and silver, so that they may present to the Lord [grain] offerings in righteousness."
Malachi 3:2-3

Even those whose entire life and heritage were centered around purity and holiness are not righteous enough to come close. **The thoughts and intents of the heart, unseen by everyone around, must become completely in line with The God who speaks from the midst of the fire.** As these are shaped and refined by Holy Spirit, you will become the inheritance of God and the inheritor of The Kingdom, a "Burning One". This is who He is calling you out to become. Come out of hiding in the wilderness to the pathway that you may be shaped into the pure, mighty weapon that God has designed you to be. Make the enemy shake in his boots as you come forth in the presence and power of God to step into the promise and inheritance in The Kingdom!

> *- Everything of true value must pass through the fire.*

> *"...I counsel you to buy from Me gold refined in the fire, that you may be rich; and white garments, that you may be clothed, that the shame of your nakedness may not be revealed; and anoint your eyes with eye salve, that you may see. As many as I love, I rebuke and chasten. Therefore be zealous and repent..."*
> **Revelation 3:18-19**

The gold, in this context, speaks of eternally valued purity in the eyes of The Lord. All the outward duties, rules, and regulations that you follow to "be good" are nothing unless they are tried by the fire. The thoughts and intentions of the heart must be from selfless love and devotion to The King and His Kingdom and not for your own benefit or to make yourself feel better. **The Fire of God will reveal the gold that is in you.** With this pure value, as you bring it to the Lord and give yourself sacrificially, you are able to invest in The Kingdom and gain an immediate return which is more golden identity and divine destiny, removal of all stain of iniquity and robes of righteousness, and anointed vision for yourself and others.

This verse continues with the words *"Be zealous"*. It is disheartening that many in the religious system try to quench the zeal in individuals. The passion and emotion of a new believer should not be put out, but fueled. The passions of The Lord are what keep you from becoming stale, boring, and dried up. **Passion and emotion must be refined, but this means turning the heat up, not putting out the fire.**

Zeal and passion will lead you to repent when mistakes are made, because you do not want anything to get in the way of your fresh relationship with The Lord. **You should never be afraid to be real, raw, and honest with God because He sees your heart no matter how you may try to hide it.** The only thing that happens when you mute your emotions is that you build a wall to keep yourself away from the presence of The Lord.

It is time to break down every wall of separation. You do this through repentance that you may be restored and refined more into the image of God. Here, the message is *"be zealous and repent!!!"* These are not mutually exclusive, but fuel each other that you may come closer than ever before.

If you continue reading after the quoted passage, repentance brings a knocking and invitation to open the door that has not been opened before. **You are invited to a deeper, more intimate place with Jesus than ever before as you walk in repentance and passion.** Jesus does not just want to come in to advise you and correct you, He desires to sit and dine with you.

True intimacy is available to those who are willing to inhabit the fire of purification and admit their need for refining in a real and honest way. It is not easy to live in this place, but here, you will gain the reward of sitting, dining, and communing with Jesus as an overcomer and ruler in The Kingdom as a "Burning One!"

- Purification must come to the sons and daughters of God.

"...Then one of the seraphim flew to me, having in his hand a live coal which he had taken with the tongs from the altar. And he touched my mouth with it, and said: 'Behold, this has touched your lips; Your iniquity is taken away, And your sin purged.' Also I heard the voice of the Lord, saying: 'Whom shall I send, And who

will go for Us?' Then I said, 'Here am I! Send me.'"
Isaiah 6:1-8

When you see The Lord, you will be changed. When you are open and receptive to receive all He has for you a burning fire will be offered to you as a gift. **You have the choice to submit, receive, and advance or resist and remain the same. You must be changed into the image of God to receive all He has for you!**

The Word of The Lord is a fire to bring purification, and draw you deeper. This can only happen by repentance and obedience. The fire burns and reveals the hidden pollution in your life. You can hold on to this filth and remain in the same place with the same people. However, if you have trained yourself to hear The Word and receive it, you will be joined together with this fiery catalyst and purged of any contamination by offering your tainted vessel as a willing sacrifice. This repentance will lead to further refining of your heart and desires and a new pathway to receive.

Here, Isaiah's ears were open to supernatural conversations that had never been heard before. Now, his focus is no longer on himself or his own inadequacies, but on receiving and carrying out the desires of the only One worthy. He immediately volunteers completely and unconditionally for the unknown action that is being discussed. At this moment, **his hunger has pushed him through the fiery forge of purging and purification and into the very frontline of volunteering for a mission he is ill-equipped and unqualified for.** He has been burned by the fire, and he will never be the same because he has become a "Burning One."

How about you?

The Fire of God will change you. As you are repeatedly ushered into the forge of His fire over and over again, you will be refined and transformed. This is increasingly unpleasant and uncomfortable in every way. What was once acceptable is no longer tolerable. People around you will laugh and mock at your stringent super-religious attitude and actions. Friends and family may no longer be able to be around the fresh fire that you are carrying. Instead of going along with the crowd now you will be singled out as a fish out of water.

Is it worth it to you?

The "hungry ones" are persecuted by the fat and lazy. The "Burning Ones" are ridiculed by the cold and comfortable. However, **those who stand back and stay the same will never be able to access the secret places, mysteries, or hidden treasure of The Kingdom.**

In the military the lowest rank, the private, does whatever he is told. He receives no important information. If he begins to ask questions he is told "that is classified". It is time to rank up in The Spirit to receive the classified information and the spiritual secrets that are only accessible the closer you come to The Lord. **This promotion will not be based on what you do but on your sacrifice and submission to The Fire of God.**

Where are the hungry people of God who are willing to light their entire being on fire with the eternal, unchanging Fire of God?

Where are those who will continually submit to the fiery forge of refining and ceaseless sacrifice of the creature comforts of the world?

These are the ones who will be purified and made ready to become the bride of Christ and receive the deep things of The Spirit.

These are the one who will become true warriors and receive the instructions of Heaven to build The Kingdom of God!!!

True purification and consecration will always lead to deeper relationship. **Deeper relationship with The Father will always call you to action!!!**

CHAPTER 5
ARMING WARRIORS

L IKE MOST YOUNG men, during college I was seriously thinking about joining the military. This has always been the way my mind has worked and was attractive to a young, energetic Texas-born male. After taking the placement test and talking with the recruiter, he said I was too intelligent for most of the jobs. He then suggested the computer hacker or possibly a chaplain because of my faith. I rejected both these ideas and decided the military was not for me. There was no way I was going to join up with the military and not be able to carry a gun. I wanted to be where the fighting and action was. It is the same way in The Spirit.

Many people of God are coming into the army of God and are not carrying any weapons. They are unprepared for the battle raging all around them because they have not been armed with the necessary armaments for their battles and missions.

It is time for a change! As hunger draws you into the presence of The Lord and His Forge burns away the unnecessary things, He is revealing your identity and transforming you into His weapon of war. **It is time to arm yourself man and woman of God with the ancient relics that**

have wreaked havoc on the enemy's forces for generations. It is time to become the armament of The Lord!!!

> *"You are My battle-ax and weapons of war: For with you I will break the nation in pieces; With you I will destroy kingdoms..."*
> *Jeremiah 51:20-23*

The destiny that God has for you is far greater than you could imagine. In chapter one of this passage, Jeremiah is telling God that he is too young and not able to fulfill what God has for him. Jeremiah was obedient to walk out what God had called him to and the fire of The Word of God burns within him. Here, God is expanding his vision again to overtake nations and kingdoms. **Time spent in The Wilderness Way, seeking The Lord and drawing close to Him has been training, forging, and arming this man of God to be used beyond his limited capacity.**

Think of it this way, someone with a knife is dangerous. Give them a sword and maybe they become a little more threatening. More training can cause them to be more effective, but give that person a gun, and they will level up in their deadliness. If you take that same person and put them in a tank, they will blow past the defense of a thousand people with knives and swords. God wants to level you and your gear up in such a way that you become an unstoppable force for His Kingdom.

The forge is where this process takes place. In the midst of the Wilderness Way is a place of testing and trials. This furnace of affliction is not just where the fire of God is, but where the wind of The Holy Spirit blows on this fire and you become red-hot for Him and are transformed into a Burning One. The oil of His presence fuels the red-hot ember, and this is the warrior's forge.

You are being shaped and molded that you may become truly effective and totally usable!

The more you step into the forge, the more you are able to become a new *"battle axe and weapon of war"* in The Master's Hand, an instrument of righteousness for His glory!!!

> *"... do not present your members as instruments of unrighteousness to sin, but present yourselves to God as being alive from the dead, and your members as instruments of righteousness to God..."* **Romans 6:12-14** *NKJV*

What does it mean to be an instrument of righteousness?

Being raised in the church, I know all the stuff that you are supposed to do. The religious rules to follow that make you look good. When I was younger, my parents were so proud that I would bring a few coins to put in the offering each week at church. I did this faithfully for many weeks and their admiration for me grew. This continued for a long time until my older brother came in one day and said "Hey, why is there no more silver in my piggy bank?" I had systematically replaced the nickels, dimes, and quarters in his piggy bank with pennies so that I could bring a more acceptable offering to church.

This is a true story that I hope caused you to laugh, but *how many times is this done in The Spirit?* A certain action causes you to receive glory or acceptance in the eyes of man, and you do it for them to see and recognize. However, you are not really giving anything of worth, but trading in the value of others. **You cannot fake it in the forge.** You cannot falsify righteousness. You cannot wear your nice church clothes, and mask, on Sunday and then return to your worldly ways the rest of the week.

Most people know how they should act, the way they should talk, and what is required to be a "Christian." Read the Bible, pray, give, spend time with Jesus, worship... They know the thoughts and attitudes, but it is rare for anyone to begin to systematically apply these to their daily lives. **The armaments of The Lord become relics because they are unused by the common man.** Weaponless warriors go into battle everyday and wonder why they are constantly walking in defeat.

Righteousness is every single day. There is no time off. It is quite controversial when you begin to apply what the Bible actually says with that which has been ingrained by the worldly system.

Do the movies you watch and the music you listen to affect your spiritual life? That is just personal conviction. It does not affect me.

Do you pray and read your Bible every day? I really don't have time to do that.

Do you give a tithe to The Lord? I cannot really afford to do that right now.

Most soldiers cannot get past basic training to the big guns because they do not apply The Word of God and walk in The Way.

Advanced training is for those who complete basic and progress on. Soldiers will never forget or leave this training behind, but this training must be built upon, and honed into a greater more efficient and specific design for each troop's specific designation. **The more you train, the more dangerous you become!** Even the most advanced and equipped soldier will spend his free time training, for he knows that the way he lives each day prepares him for the unexpected emergency situations that require his particular expertise.

Many promises of The Lord are sitting waiting to be wielded and are wasting away because of abandonment and disuse. These weapons are *"not physical [weapons of flesh and blood]. Our weapons are divinely powerful for the destruction of fortresses"* (**2 Corinthians 10:4**).

True warriors have applied themselves continually to basic training and are ready to begin instruction on more advanced weaponry while never forgetting the fundamentals. I will only speak of a few of these things here, but a myriad of new and exciting tools are accessible to those who are walking with Holy Spirit.

WARRIOR WEAPONS

Every warrior has access to every spiritual weapon in the armory of God. Some may be used more than others. The weapons noted here are those mentioned in scripture and how they are used in the indicated verses. This is to whet your appetite for what is available to lay hold of in the spiritual realm. Do not make a theology or a doctrine around any of these things, but use them to study the principles, promises, and power that you, as a warrior, have access to as you walk in The Wilderness Way and begin to advance into The Promise!

- Sword

The sword is for protection and guarding against danger (*Gen 3, Sol 3:8*). The enemy will come to pilfer anything that he can. The sword is The Word of God. As you speak out The Word you are protected and guarded against the destruction the enemy would try to cause.

The sword is for taking inheritance (*Gen 48:22*). Israel battled with his sword and bow to take the inheritance that he is passing down to his grandchildren. You will take your inheritance as you line yourself up with The Word.

The sword is for taking possession (*Exod 15:9*). The enemy thought to destroy the people of God and repossess those whom God had freed. They were trying to take possession but this was reversed at the Red Sea as the Israelites took their first steps into a promise of freedom.

The sword of The Lord reveals the already fallen enemies (*Lev 26:37*). The enemies that are coming against you have already been defeated. You must step into the power that you have been given.

The sword is for righteous judgment (*Deut 13:15*). Every unholy thought and action will be judged by The Standard, Jesus. Anything that does not line up with Him and His character will pass away.

The drawn sword is the readiness to advance (*Josh 5:13*). The warrior's sword is not sheathed but drawn to advance The Kingdom in every area.

The sword is power (*1 Sam 17*). The power of man is nothing compared to the sword of The Lord. Proclaim the Word of The Lord and walk in His power.

The sword is for battle and war (*2 Sam 12*). The warrior has not been born to sleep and be lazy, but to fight against the enemy.

The sword is sharp and effective for daily battle (*Ezek 21:9-10*). A warrior's sword must be kept ready and honed for ultimate effectiveness. The ready warrior is one who has kept his blade in a constant condition of readiness for immediate action.

The sword is a weapon and a tool. Used in times of war and and in times of harvesting (*Joel 3, Micah 4*). It is both defensive and offensive. The sword is a tool for harvesting the crops at the proper time to produce provision. It is necessary in times of war, harvest, and all the times in between.

The sword, the Word of God, is living and active (*Heb 4:12*). It is not some dormant, sleeping thing. As soon as it is taken up and put into practice it is useful and effective for war and bringing in a fruitful harvest. The Word is only ineffective when you do not speak it out or line up your life with it.

- Rod/staff

The staff is wielded for judgment and reversal of enemy attack. Even the sharp weapon of the enemy cannot defeat the club or rod in the hand of God's warrior (*2 Sam 23:21*). The authority that is given to you through Christ will overcome every "spectacular" enemy.

The rod is for the family leader (*Num 17*). Whether you have a physical family or not, when you take up the rod of God, you become empowered to be a generational leader in The Kingdom.

The rod is for discipline and correction (*2 Sam 7:14, 1 Cor 4:21*). A father will discipline his son for correction, but those not in the family will receive the rod of judgment.

The rod is for beating out cumin (*Isa 28:27*). *Why is this important?* Cumin was valued for its healing qualities. Black cumin was thought to be a cure for heart disease. The discipline, correction, and guiding of the rod will lead to a healed and whole heart.

The rod breaks through hardness (*Psalm 2*). This breakthrough is not just for individuals, but entire nations that have been continually made hard and resistant by the schemes of the enemy. The rod is able to break through this hardness so that the light of The Gospel can bring transformation.

The rod is a comfort and strength (*Psalm 23*). For the sons, the rod is a safe security that God is shepherding and guiding them on the proper path to the promise. Wrong paths in the wilderness may lead to destruction, but the rod directs you to walk in The Wilderness Way.

Passing under the rod means that you are counted as one of the flock (*Ezek 20:37*). Those outside of the correction and direction of The Lord are not a part of the flock. They will not walk in The Way or follow Him.

The rod is for measurement (**Ezek 40**). Your thoughts, actions, and life are measured by the standard of Jesus. The things that are built upon the foundation will be measured by the rod of God so they may stand the test of time.

The rod of the son is fruit bearing (*Num 17*). Aaron's rod budded and bore fruit when it was entirely impossible. However, when you are properly positioned with the Lord, you will bear fruit.

The rod is a generational legacy, inheritance, and blessing (*Heb 11:21, Gen 49*). Jacob leaned on his staff and blessed each one of his sons speaking blessings prophetically for generations to come. This staff was a symbol of what was being passed down in the spirit and the father's blessing that was being declared. When you walk with the rod of God, not only will you receive divine blessings of generations past, but you will be able to multiply this blessing to the generations that will come after you.

- Hammer

The hammer is for work (*Exodus 25:18, 37:17*). It is a tool as well as a weapon. The work being done to construct the tabernacle is of hammered gold. It takes skill to wield a hammer both as a craftsmen and as a warrior.

The hammer is used in conjunction with the tent peg (*Judges 4, 5*). These are used to expand and stretch forth the territory of the user.

The hammer is for building (*1 Kings 6*). The building of the tabernacle took stone that was hammered and chiseled outside of the temple. Work was done on the stone outside of the temple that it could be fit together in the presence of the altar.

The hammer is for breaking (*Psalm 74:6*). The things not of The Lord are broken down by the hammer. The hard, resistant to change, things must be broken down so that the new, shapeable materials can be used. The understanding of both the breaking down of the old and the building up of the new is contained within this weapon and tool of the warrior.

The hammer is for change (*Jer 23:29*). The word of The Lord is a hammer. The ways of the world must be broken down and removed. Strongholds and illegal structures of religion must be destroyed so that The Kingdom can be built up. The hammer is not to destroy people, but to make a way so that the new righteous building may be properly positioned. The hammer is used to build and finely craft the work of The Lord and bring glory to His name.

- *Battle Axe*

The axe is used for work to cut trees (*Deut 19:5*). The axe was primarily a tool used for day to day work. The cutting of trees for firewood and clearing land would have made this a rather common tool for every individual. When it came time for battle, this would have been a weapon that any common man would have been comfortable wielding because of their familiarity with it in their day to day life.

The axe was not used for cutting down fruit bearing trees (*Deut 20*). This was specifically mentioned even during war and siege time. Fruit was highly valued and was not to be disturbed but continually harvested, even and especially, in times of war. In the same way, you must be careful that the harvest is not harmed whether you are planting and sowing or breaking and building. The harvest must be protected at all cost.

The axe is used to cut trees for fuel (*Judges 9*). Fuel for the fire to continue was important. The axe was for continual clearing, but never wasting. Just as fruit and the harvest was vitally important, so was fuel. Nothing must be wasted, but fuel for the fire must be constantly replenished.

The axe was used for various other types of work (*2 Sam 12*). Here, they used axes to dig out clay to make bricks. The axe was a multi tool that could be fitted with different heads for different tasks. It was for work as well as for war, and would have been the tool of the common man.

The axe was made of iron (*2 Kings 6*). This was meant for strength and the ability to be used repeatedly over long periods of time. The nature of the axe was not to float, but supernaturally God allowed this to happen. God blessed the work of those who are His and helps them continue to completion as they keep coming back to Him for help and strength.

The axe must be used with wisdom and strength working together (*Eccl 10:10*). The axe can demolish and destroy, but it can also clear land and provide fuel. Wisdom keeps the axe sharp and efficient for use. Strength is necessary for application, but without wisdom, more strength will be required to do the same amount of work. Wisdom brings efficiency when wielding the axe.

The axe must be wielded by The Master (*Isa 10:15*). God is the primary Axeman. He will use you as an axe for His glory as you wield it for His purpose. Wisdom to hear and obey will keep you properly aligned with His plan and purpose and keep you from destroying the harvest.

The axe is designed to humble the proud and arrogant as The Mighty One wields it (*Isa 10:33-34*). God uses the axe to bring low those that have built themselves up. God will show his supremacy, not by exalting Himself, but destroying the buildings that have been erected illegally and unrighteously. Those who trust in God will be exalted. Those who are proud of what they have built themselves will be humbled.

The axe is used to destroy the serpent, Egypt (*Jer 46:22*). As stated before, Egypt means double bondage. The axe is used against this slimy serpent to completely cut off and sever the head as well as every attachment that would try to bring people into bondage or subjugation to it. The mind and body will be freed from this control as the axe is wielded to destroy it.

The battle axe is used as a weapon of war for shattering and destroying the enemies of God (*Jer 51:19-23*). When judgment comes upon the adversaries of The Lord, the battle axe will completely demolish the enemy and every evil work that he has planned.

The axe is used for final judgment (*Ezek 9*). Those who have been given the opportunity to repent but have completely rejected and adamantly opposed The Lord and walked contrary to His commands will be judged. The axe is used for final judgment against all those who have made themselves enemies of The Lord.

The axe is used to judge those who do not bear fruit, especially the religious spirit (*Matt 3:10, Luke 3:9*). The tree is bad if the fruit is bad, but if the root is left in the ground, the tree may spring up again. The axe of The Lord is against the very root of all those things that would spring up and appear good, but have been poisoned. These must be completely uprooted and thrown into the fire.

- Spear

The spear is the glory of a warrior (*1 Chr 11:23*). The giant was impressive until the spear was taken away. Then Benaiah got the glory when he killed him with his own spear.

The spear is for righteousness (*Num 25:8*). This weapon was used to stop unrighteousness from destroying the people of God.

The spear is authority (*Josh 8:18*). As Joshua points his spear at Ai, the people who had easily defeated them before, because of sin in the camp, are completely overcome. God had given them the authority to defeat the enemy where they had once lost it.

The spear is for warfare (*Judges 5:8*). In the song of Deborah and Barak, they are recounting the history of the people of God. When false gods began to arise and steal away the hearts of the people, no one rose to war against them with shield or spear. They sat back and were overtaken because no one arose to stand against these demonic idols.

The spear is for strength (*1 Sam 17:7, 45-47, 26:11-12*). Goliath was impressive because of the weight of the spear he carried in the physical, that is why it is specifically mentioned. When David comes, he does not even bring a spear in the physical because he knows that The Name of The Lord is his weapon. God delivers by His words not by physical weapons. The Name and word of The Lord are far more powerful than the strength of man.

The spear is for power (*Joel 3:10*). Preparing for war, the people transformed their pruning hooks into spears that they might be ready for battle. The implements of harvest that were already accessible were transformed into weapons that would give them power to defeat the enemy in battle.

The spear is preparing for war and impending battle. (*Job 39:23, Jer*

46:4). The polished and gleaming spear shows that the warrior is ready for battle. He is not hiding but has sharpened and is ready to meet the enemy with strength and power.

The spear is for piercing (*John 19:34*). The warrior uses the spear to pierce into the inward parts. The Word of The Lord goes down deep and pierces through the hard exterior to effect change in the inward parts.

The spear is used for war or hunting big, dangerous game. In antiquity, the spear was the weapon of choice for hunting mammoth and buffalo. These were dangerous beasts that could slay anyone that got close. The spear extended their reach and was more effective in piercing thick hide than arrows.

The spear is the weapon that God used to turn the enemies own weapons against them (*Hab 3:14*). During battle, God pierces the head of the enemy with his own devices. The supposed power of the enemy is easily overcome by The Almighty and used to defeat him.

The spear is used as a gleaming, glittering and flashing weapon. It is a lightning of God used as revelation for children and confusion for the enemy (*Hab 3:11*). This chapter in *Habakkuk* outlines many of aspects of the spear of The Lord. His splendor, majesty, power, salvation and destruction of the enemy, strength and security of The Lord are all attributes of The Lord represented by the spear.

In times of peace, the spear is transformed into a pruning hook (*Isa 2:4*). The strength and glory of the spear is used only for war and battle. In times of rest and peace, the spear is for pruning away the unrighteous, impure things.

Pruning and the use of the pruning hook are signs of peace and prosperity. Lack of pruning describes desolation (*Isa 5:6*). Without pruning and purifying, the life of the people of God will become desolate and wasted.

- Bow and Arrow

The bow is used for hunting food (**Gen 27:3**). Daily provision would have made it necessary to be proficient in the shooting of arrows.

The arrows of the Lord are used to shatter the supposed strength of His enemies (**Num 24:8**). The pride and might that is found within them will be crushed as the arrows of The Lord go forth.

The arrows of The Lord are judgment for disobedience (**Deut 32:23**). Rebellion and disobedience of the people will lead to judgment. The blessings of The Lord were attributed to idols, and His loving commands were rejected. The arrows were swift and just judgment on disobedience in order to turn His people back to Him, that they might be saved.

The arrows of The Lord are the utterances of His voice that scatters every enemy and unrighteous person (**2 Sam 22:14-15**). The arrows are here paralleled with the lightning of God. Confusion and scattering comes from the arrows of light, the words that come from The Most High.

The arrows of The Lord are victory (**2 Kings 13:15-19**). As the king came into line with The Word of The Lord, the arrows proclaimed the victory over the enemy. To the extent that he was obedient to The Lord, this is the same measure that he gained the victory over the enemy.

The arrows represented courageous and mighty warriors (**1 Chr 12:2**). They knew how to wield a bow and shoot arrows from either hand. This made them powerful and dangerous in a way that most would not be. This was a unique ability to effectively use the weapons to the fullest.

The arrows of fire are judgment for the unrepentant ones (**Psalm 7:12-13**). God is just and gives every opportunity for the one walking outside of His will to return to Him. However, those who continually reject the commands and warnings of The Lord are pronouncing judgment upon themselves. The Fire of purity will come upon those who continually turn their backs on Him.

The arrows of The Almighty will scatter, confuse, and defeat every strong enemy (*Psalm 18:14*). Though many may come against the Word and Revelation of The Lord, these enemies cannot overcome or overwhelm the thunderings and utterances that come straight from Him.

The arrows of The Lord are sharp and piercing (*Psalm 45:5*). As the Lord speaks forth His Word, the enemies are pierced to the heart with The Truth, and unrighteousness is revealed.

The arrows are the lightning of God (*Psalm 77:17*). God thunders from heaven and speaks, and lightning revelation comes forth as arrows and illuminates the people of God.

Arrows are equated with words (*Psalm 64:3*). Enemies will sharpen their tongues as arrows and aim poisonous slander, gossip, and lies at the people of God. However, The Truth will destroy every lie and uproot every evil plot. The voice of The Lord will burn up every dark scheme against the people of God.

The arrows are the warrior's weapon (*Psalm 120:4*). The words of The Lord that come forth from the warrior declarations are sharp and flaming instruments against His enemies.

The arrows of The Lord are confusion, embarrassment, and frustration for the enemy (*Psalm 144:6*). The declaration of The Lord dispels every dark and deceitful thing. The enemy's plots and schemes are revealed and brought to disarray at The Word of The Lord.

The warrior has been made into the sharp arrow of The Lord (*Isa 49:2*). When you allow The Word of The Lord to purify, refine, and forge you, you will speak His Word and become the weapon hidden in His quiver. You will be ready to be sent forth with The Truth into every dark stronghold and destroy the work of every enemy.

- Sling

The sling is used to hurl out and disperse every enemy that would come against the warrior. (*1 Sam 25:29, Jer 10:18*). The enemy will be routed, confused, and cast far from the people of God who stand in His presence. He will be flung far away never to return and trouble the land again.

The sling and stone are used for destroying every enemy work and structure (*2 Kings 3:25*). The works of the enemy will be surrounded, cut off, and completely destroyed by the people of God.

The sling and stone is a warrior's weapon (*1 Chr 12:2*). Those skilled in long range warfare will be able to destroy the enemy from a long distance by declaring The Word of The Lord and speaking forth His promises.

The sling is for triumph even when there is no proper weapon in the hand of the son (*1 Sam 17:50*). The promises of The Lord in the hands of a son will destroy every enemy giant whether there is a proven weapon in their hand or not. The promises will overcome, and they will receive the power to cut off the head of the enemy as they advance.

- Stone

The stone is partnered with the sling, but has its own nature and components.

The stone is used as building material (*Gen 11:3*). The bricks made by man were equated with the stone that had already been created. The stone is eternal and outlasts the works of mankind.

The stone was used as a monument and memorial (*Gen 28:22*). It was an unchanging, everlasting reminder of a word or promise of The Lord.

The stone was used as an eternal testimony, witness, and memorial

(*Gen 31:45*). The memorial is a reminder of what was said or done at that place at a certain point in time.

The stone is shown here to be the eternal strength of The Shepherd of Israel (*Gen 49:24*). God represents Himself as The Stone of Israel.

The stones are living testimonies (*1 Pet 2:4-5*). Jesus was the living testimony given from heaven. Now, you are a living stone, an eternal testimony to the power, purpose, and promise of God on the earth. Each living testimony is being built into the eternal dwelling place of The Lord. A stone is a testimony that continues to speak throughout all eternity. What you have witnessed and been changed by speaks of a Living, Eternal God. As you continue to be changed and continue to speak, you are the living testimony. A testimony is not a one time thing. A testimony forgotten will be wasted. A promise unremembered becomes powerless. However, **promises spoken and declared are power-filled and active for generations to come.** The true testimony of The Lord is alive and will last forever.

A memorial is a specific event that happened in the past that reminds of a promise completed. **The testimony speaks of the ongoing, continuing promise of an everlasting God Who is with you, continually fulfilling His eternal promises.**

When David chose five stones in *1 Samuel 17*, these were specific testimonies of Who God is and what He had done. These declared the power of The Lord to do it again and greater. The faith of David that defeated the giant was that which God had said and done in the past, He would do again, accomplishing even greater works, because He had grabbed ahold of the power of the eternal testimony and promise.

UNCOMMON WEAPONS

The most common weapons have been discussed, but there are several not so common ones that are worth mentioning.

- Battering Ram

The battering ram is used to break open walls of the unrighteous kingdom (*Ezek 26:9*). Anything that exalts itself against The Lord must be laid waste.

The battering ram is used to break open gates (*Ezek 4:2*). An unrepentant city under judgment will be overcome by The Almighty Righteous One. Open the gates that the King of Glory may come in (*Psalm 24:7*).

- Threshing Sledge

The threshing sledge brings pressure but does not crush (*Isa 41:15-20*). The threshing sledge beats out the harvest that leads to righteousness. It brings holiness for the fruit of The Lord, and judgment for the chaff. The threshing sledge creates a threshold of separation and distinction (*1 Cor 9:10*). A threshold is a point of entry for the blessing of The Lord, and points to the harvest of fruit.

The threshold is also a point of judgment on worthless, unrighteous, or temporary things. The waste is separated from the seed of the harvest and the fruit by the threshing sledge.

- Jawbone

The jawbone is an unlikely, unexpected instrument for judgment on the enemy (*Judges 15:15-17*). Speaking out and declaring the victory seems like an unlikely way to gain the victory. The glory of God is revealed in the unexpected victories with special circumstances.

The power of the enemy is wrapped up in his jawbone or the false words he declares (*Ezek 29:3-7*). The power of prideful words and lying lips spoken by an enslaving enemy will be broken by the people of God declaring The Word of The Lord and the power of The Promise.

- Millstone

The millstone is used for the crushing of wheat that produces flour for bread (*Deut 24:6*). This was not a primary weapon but an instrument to bring forth bread.

The millstone is a common harvesting implement that is used to crush the head of the enemy who comes with unholy fire to destroy (*Judges 9:53*). The judgment and crushing of the enemy was by an unlikely weapon wielded by an unlikely person but brought about great victory for the city.

The millstone is made of stone and used to describe the heart of leviathan (*Job 41:24*). It is hard and very weighty.

The millstone was a sign of slavery or servitude (*Isa 47:2*). As you give yourself completely to the service of The Lord, you will be used to cut out the prideful heart of the leviathan, bring forth a harvest, and crush the head of the enemy.

The millstone is the total destruction of a great enemy (*Rev 18:21*). The work of the enemy will cease as the people of God bring glory and honor to The Lord.

- Ox Goad

The answer to the prayers of people was a man with a ranch tool (*Judges 3:31*). Shamgar is mentioned twice in the Bible, and his name means sword. The people prayed for deliverance. Their cries for freedom were answered by a simple rancher who placed himself in the presence of God to be used by Him. In doing this, what was in his hand became a tool of deliverance as he was empowered by the Almighty.

- Tent Peg

A simple woman who served The Lord became an instrument of deliverance with the common working tool, a tent peg (*Judges 4:21, 5:26*). The tent peg is for multiplication and expansion (*Isa 54:2*). As the people moved and expanded territory, they would make their tent pegs fit the new places they would camp.

The tent pegs were used in the normal way of life (*Num 4:29-33*). They were taken up, moved and put down every time it came to move in the wilderness.

Jesus is the tent peg, the expansion and place of security in normal life. At the same time, he is The Mighty Warrior expanding and occupying every enemy territory (*Zech 10:4*).

Wherever you may be and whatever you may be doing at the moment, God has placed something in your hand that can be used for His glory and the deliverance of His people. As you place yourself into complete obedience of The Almighty, anything you have, whether common or special, will be used to bring Him glory!

- Bare Hands

The deliverance of the people of God came about from Egypt even though they had nothing in their hands (*Deut 4:34*). The signs and wonders by the hand of God caused the people to be freed even though all they had was bare hands. As they went out, they did not go out empty-handed but their enemy came out to them with heaps of treasure. The absence of a weapon allowed them the freedom to carry off the spoils of war.

The king and mighty warriors were given into the bare hands of Joshua (*Josh 6:2*). As he walked in obedience, even when it did not make any sense militarily, God gave him, and the people of God, the entire city without a battle.

God is your rock and strength, and He is the one who trains your hands for battle (*Psalm 144:1*). As you draw near to Him, He strengthens and empowers you to do His work with whatever may or may not be in your hand. You become the weapon of war in His hands by your submission and obedience.

THE ARMOR

"Therefore take up the whole armor of God, that you may be able to withstand in the evil day, and having done all, to stand. Stand therefore..." Ephesians 6:13-14 NKJV

You are commanded to take up the whole armor of God. Without the armor, you are naked and unprotected in a battle that has been raging since before time began. Paul's encouragement outlines some of the equipment you can use in your day to day battle. These are not physical objects, but spiritually applied, each of these things are both defensive and offensive in the war against the evil one.

- *"Be strong in The Lord and in the power of His might"* (**vs.10**)

By yourself, you have no power over spiritual things. You are weak and helpless even if you are strong in mind and body. The strength of this world will not help you when fighting spiritual battles. You are called to draw on the strength of The Lord as your source. Spending time in His presence will revive, restore, re-energize and strengthen you in a way nothing else can. Religious requirements and legalistic laws are limited by those who created them. The Creator of the universe has unlimited strength and power that He freely offers to all those who look to Him as their source. **This is where all warriors must start, at the feet of Jesus, so He can raise you up to be seated in heavenly places with Him.**

- *Stand firm*

You are called not just to stand during the battle, but to stand firm. Hold the line and never give up an inch. We are to be continually holding fast and advancing in every area. We do not retreat or surrender.

We must war and fight to enter into The Kingdom right here, right now. Labor to enter the rest.

- Armor helps you to stand

In the midst of a raging battle you are told over and over again to stand firm. Jesus has won the victory in the past as well as the future. In the present, you may not have seen it take place yet, but you are called to stand on the firm foundation of the promises of God. Perseverance and patient persistence will cause you to overcome the enemy no matter what your senses may tell you.

Resources from The Commander will reach you shortly if you do not give up or surrender. **You are an overcomer! To win, you must never retreat but stand firm and advance as opportunity arises.**

- The fight is in heavenly places

Too many times you can look at the situations around you and find those who might be considered enemies. In the end, the battle is in heavenly places. It is a spiritual battle with godly weapons in heavenly places. Do not let the issues of this life drag you down to their level.

- Gird your waist with truth

"What is truth" (*John 18:38*)? This is a question Pilate asked Jesus in the midst of his pre-crucifixion trial. All the other issues boiled down to this.

The world would have you to believe that each person can create their own truth and so determine their own reality. *However, what happens when my truth opposes your truth?* Currently whoever is louder and convinces more people to join them becomes the speaker of truth.

The mob or majority determines the truth and reality for the rest of society. If you disagree, they silence you through intimidation or force so that you can never become the majority or loudest to sway people to your side. This is not a new concept. This did not work out so well for the people of Israel (see *Judges 19-21*). This is how the book of *Judges* concludes:

"In those days... every man did what was right in his own eyes."
Judges 21:25

"You do you, Bro!" "What is your truth?" These things are heard so often in today's culture because the world has gotten off track. Without one standard of truth, right and wrong is subjective, and you can essentially do whatever your flesh desires. The works of the flesh lead to pain, destruction, and death (*Romans 7:5*).

The people of God are called to wear The Truth around their waist as a decorated and ornate belt. If you are ever in Texas, you have probably seen some humongous belt buckles. Cowboys are proud of their culture. This is how you are instructed to have The Truth of God, evident for all to see. It keeps you from being exposed and guards your ability to spiritually reproduce properly.

Jesus said in *John 14:6*, "*I am The Way, The Truth, and The Life...*". This should end all dispute about what the standard of truth is. **Jesus is the standard. There is no personal truth, only The Truth that is revealed by the person of Jesus.** As you walk with Him, you are walking in The Truth. He should be proudly displayed for all to see. This is the protection you have against the lies of the enemy. Jesus, and The Truth that He is, will destroy every lie the enemy brings up to hurt you.

- Put on the breastplate of righteousness

In a society where truth is relative, righteousness, purity, and holiness are almost bad words. The world unilaterally wants no standards so that conviction and shame, that would lead to repentance, will never come. The righteousness of God is to be a breastplate that shields the presence of Holy Spirit flowing in and out of us. It is the protector of our heart and emotions, and keeper of our well of life, out of which everything else flows. Pure rivers of living water will stream out of our bellies if they are protected from the potential poisoning of the enemy.

"For He made Him who knew no sin to be sin for us, that we might become the righteousness of God in Him."
2 Corinthians 5:21 *NKJV*

Only through Jesus and His sacrifice are you able to step into full righteousness. On your own, you can only walk in rules, regulations, and religion which will never completely set you free but bring a new type of bondage. Jesus paid the price that all those who walk in Him may be made righteous and walk with Him like they never could before.

- Shod your feet with the preparation of the gospel of peace

The good news is ever advancing and forever going forth. It is the revelation that you can be truly whole and complete in the presence of your Maker. Your Creator knows you and is the only One who can lead you into your eternal destiny. Your original design can only be found as you come close to The Presence. This revelation and knowledge must be carried throughout the earth upon the feet of the warrior. *"We are not of those who draw back in fear, but we are of those who press in to the salvation, healing, and freedom of the soul"* (**Hebrews 10:39**)!!!

The peace that surpasses understanding will guard you from the storms and trials of this life. Just as God has His forge in the Wilderness Way so the enemy has a counterfeit. His demonic fire is to hurt, burn, and destroy. It may seem pleasant at first, but will consume you quickly if you give yourself to the ways of the world. The enemy's flaming darts are constantly being flung to destroy what God has built. You must become a Burning One, forged by The Fire of God. Even when you walk through the fire of the enemy, you will not be burned for He is with you and protects you from the enemy's attempts to hinder the advancement of The Kingdom.

- Take the shield of faith with which you will be able to quench all the fiery darts of the wicked one

You are not to rush forward in blind faith, but you have the sure and secure confidence that Jesus is with you. He will fulfill every promise He has spoken and caused to be written in His Word. Your faith will allow you to destroy every lie of the enemy that would question the character or utterance of The Commander. Faith is not ethereal, but firm and solid as a shield against all enemy attack. As often as he would try to distract, detract, or destroy The Word, the very worlds are being held together because of the spoken word of God. Nothing can come into existence without the spoken Word. This is something you can hold onto; God is faithful and will bring to pass everything He has said, both now and in the future.

- Take the helmet of salvation

Your mind must be grounded and rooted in The Word, and your connection with The Spirit protects you from illegally implanted schemes. You have been delivered and set free from the bondage the enemy would lead you into, and you have been given the mind of Christ. Because of this, you are able to walk into freedom having your mind constantly renewed to come into union with The Spirit (*I Corinthians 2:16*).

- Take the sword of the Spirit, which is the word of God;

The Word is a sword, a fire, a hammer, a battle axe. This is the weapon you use to combat every attack of the enemy. By The Word of God, you step up into the power and authority you have been given and begin to take the fight to the enemy.

The gates of hell will not prevail against The Word. The darkness cannot overcome the light. Jesus combatted every attack of the enemy with The Word of God. It must not only be in your mind and heart, but you must be saturated with The Living Word, the Spirit of Jesus, that you may be full of the fire of God. This is how you can walk through the fires of hell and not be burned. Because you are filled with the living, active fire of God nothing can touch or harm you.

The promises of God are sure, and He is faithful to complete them. Through faith and patient endurance you walk into your inheritance, which is The Truth that He has spoken to you and over you before you were even created. You have an eternal inheritance that has been promised to The Sons. The way you step into it is by continually declaring these words out until you see them bear fruit.

The enemy would come to snatch these seeds out of your very mouth if you let him. He will seek to cause your heart to harden because of circumstances and situations around you. The enemy will even cause distractions, cares, and worries to choke out the life that is contained in these simple words which are actually powerful promises waiting to bear fruit for all those who will diligently cultivate them. Do not let one promise fall to the ground uncultivated, but **speak out these powerful promises and watch the harvest of abundance come forth in your life, overshadowing everyone around you with plenty!**

- Pray always with all prayer and supplication in the Spirit

What is prayer? Words you say to a higher power? Communication with a divine being? **Prayer happens when you submit your entire being to a living God and walk in obedience to Him in every area.** Praise and worship are prayer. Fasting is prayer. Sweeping a floor to the glory of God is prayer. Time spent seeking the Lord is prayer. Even in your deepest darkest moments when you don't know how to pray... as you focus on Jesus, this is prayer.

Interestingly, Paul purposefully draws attention to prayer *"in The Spirit"*. *Can you pray in your flesh?* The answer must be yes. Praying in the spirit is more than speaking in tongues, although this is an important aspect and powerful part of praying.

John was *"in The Spirit on The Lord's Day"*, and he was invited to come up higher. There are levels and dimensions of seeking, abiding, and living in The Spirit that are waiting for you to discover and step into. The spiritual places are open to those who are submitted and walking in obedience, abiding within an infinite God. The more you are in The Spirit, the more you will be able to not only resist fleshly temptation, but begin to combat the enemy forces that wage war against your destiny.

> *- Be watchful to this end with all perseverance and supplication for all the saints— and for me, that utterance may be given to me*

Are you to be watchful for the enemy or focusing on what The Commander wants? You should always be looking for how you can serve The Commander in faithfulness and perseverance. Having done all to stand, stand firm. Not just for your own sake, but for The Commander's sake and for your fellow soldier's sake. You must stand with others, together in unity, against every attack and press forward to advance The Kingdom.

- I may open my mouth boldly to make known the mystery of the gospel...

The Word of God is to continue to go forth no matter what may come. The gospel is a powerful weapon against the enemy's schemes. The good news has the ability to set people free:

> *"open their eyes so that they may turn from darkness to light and from the power of Satan to God, that they may receive forgiveness and release from their sins and an inheritance among those who have been sanctified by faith in Me."'*
> *Acts 26:18*

What is this mystery anyway? The mystery is how you can be completely transformed and remade into the likeness of Christ. Not only that, you are continually being transformed even though major transformation happened at salvation. As you press deeper into the heart of The

Father and abide in The Spirit, the infinity of mystery is revealed more and more for all eternity.

> *"But we have this treasure in earthen vessels, that the excellence of the power may be of God and not of us...For we who live are always delivered to death for Jesus' sake, that the life of Jesus also may be manifested in our mortal flesh."*
> *2 Corinthians 4:7-12*

You are designed for the power of God to flow through you. The only thing that will stop this from happening is you. As a Warrior of The Way, you will come under intense attack. You may feel crushed, broken down, wounded or weary, but this is not the end of things. God's power within you empowers you to overcome every attack. Enduring and persevering within the presence of God ensures that you can never be defeated. Jesus has already won the war. It is your job to rid yourself of every fleshly weakness that would hold you back from becoming assimilated into the presence of God, in the forge. This is where your true power comes from. A chain is only as strong as its weakest link, but when you become super bonded with Christ, you will truly become unbroken!!!

THE BATTLE-READY WARRIORS

> *"... A people come, great and strong, The like of whom has never been; Nor will there ever be any such after them, Even for many successive generations. A fire devours before them, And behind them a flame burns... The Lord gives voice before His army, For His camp is very great; For strong is the One who executes His word... 'Now, therefore,' says the Lord, 'Turn to Me with all your heart, With fasting, with weeping, and with mourning." So rend your heart, and not your garments; Return to the Lord your God, For He is gracious and merciful, Slow to anger, and of great kindness; And He relents from doing harm.'"*
> *Joel 2:1-14 (NKJV)*

Strong, unyielding, and unbroken are the burning ones in the army of

The Lord. They come up from the wilderness and emerge out of the fire with a determination and drive to advance the Kingdom. These have been forged, fired, tested, and proven not only to stand firm, but also to press forward to destroy every enemy and overtake every stronghold, fortress, or enemy gate that would stand in the way of The Coming King. For them, it is not a fight, but a lifestyle of faith and surrender to The God of angel armies, The Lord of the Wilderness Warriors. In the past, one or two men or women of God have emerged and brought the message of The King "Prepare The Way!!!" Now is the time for the generation of Wilderness Warriors to forcibly break through every enemy barricade, like a wave breaking through a dam, and overcome each and every region with the power of God!!!

Now is The Time!!!

> *"The Kingdom of God suffers violence and the violent take it by force!"*
> *Matthew 11:2*

> *"The Kingdom of God is at hand!"*
> *Mark 1:15*

Nothing can stop a Wilderness Warrior that has completely laid down their own wants, desires, comforts, and concerns. What would have broken them previously, has been used by The Spirit of God to solidify determination and the drive to completely eradicate every enemy in the way of their Promised Land. They are no longer just surviving as they walk through the valley of the shadow of death, but releasing resurrection power. What was once dead will come to life and give glory to The Risen King!!!

This Warrior Generation is unlike anything ever seen before. They are timeless, fearless, unbroken, and free from the confines of the religious system. They have cast off the comforts and constraints of the world and have ascended into the atmosphere to join with all the warriors that have gone before them. They have taken up the timeless treasures and priceless relics of the past and joined them with the passions, purposes, and destinies of The Lord for this time period. This generation has begun to make heavenly reality transfer into the here and now.

The focus, purpose, and passion is Jesus!!! He is The Original Unbroken One and Warrior of The Way. The greatest power the enemy had, death, could not break this Man of War!!! He may have been down for a moment, but he was not defeated. He paid the price for you so that the war that you could not win would already be won before you came onto the battlefield. **Victory has been given to you, all you have to do is advance!**

Unintimidated, unbroken, and undefeated!!! All power and authority in Heaven and on earth has been given to Jesus, The Original Unbroken One, and He has placed His Spirit within you. You have the ability to walk unbroken as you crucify the flesh and walk in The Spirit of The Unbroken One!!!

> *"The Lord will go forth like a warrior, He will stir up His zeal like a man of war; He will shout out, yes, He will raise a war cry. He will prevail [mightily] against His enemies."*
> *Isaiah 42:13*

Many people have a picture of nice Jesus. Honestly, I think Jesus was anything but nice. He was loving and gentle, but the power and truth He walked in destroys any picture of nice in my mind.

In this revelation, the scripture describes The Almighty One as a man of war. His passion and fire were unmatched by anyone around Him. Oh, and he was not silent in the time of battle or when the moment came to speak truth. Clearly and plainly, a war cry arose to call all those who would follow His footsteps in The Way of righteousness. He is the conqueror of all His enemies, and I am on His side.

I may not be the greatest and the best warrior that has ever been, but I am standing with The King and all those who follow Him. My strength and hope is in Him alone. He is victorious and mighty in every battle and has already overcome every plan, scheme, and attack of the enemy. Because of this, I do not have to settle for walking in the ways of the world, but I am lifted up to walk in The Way that has been prepared for me.

> *"The king is not saved by the great size of his army; A warrior is not rescued by his great strength. A horse is a false hope for victory; Nor does it deliver anyone by its great strength. Behold, the eye of the Lord is upon those who fear Him [and worship Him with awe-inspired reverence and obedience], On those who hope [confidently] in His compassion and lovingkindness,"*
> **Psalm 33:16-18**

A Warrior's strength is more than the physical or even mental resistance and superiority to others. The measure of a Warrior of The Way is his love, and obedience to his commander. The depth of love is the strength of the warrior. His devotion and consistent desire to come close and know the true heart of The Commander will reveal the greatness that may have been hidden from outward appearances. **Strength comes from a heart and desire to please The One who paid the ultimate price for you.**

> *"I [the Lord] have commanded My consecrated ones, I have even called My great warriors..."*
> **Isaiah 13:3**

The commander of the battle is The One who has already won. He has defeated every enemy and completely overcome every potential defeat. Everything has been turned from darkness to light. As you are walking in obedience, you will see the full manifestation of this as it is revealed through your life.

The consecrated, holy, and set apart ones are those who are the best equipped for what lies ahead. Even though you may feel Ill-equipped or unprepared, you have been purified in the fire and set apart for this work. As you constantly place yourself in the presence of The Lord, you become one of the great warriors that God has called out, and you will see victory and triumph. All this is taking place that God may receive all glory and honor through your life as a simple, humble, and usable vessel.

> *"Through you I ascend to the highest peaks to stand strong and secure in you. You've trained me with the weapons of warfare-worship; my arms can bend a bow of bronze."*
> **Psalm 18:33-34** *(TPT)*

Only in the presence of The Lord and through intimacy with Him will you be raised to the highest heights and accelerated in the atmosphere into all that He has for you. The Warrior is trained and equipped in the pinnacle regions with the Lord. Strength and security comes from faith and trust in The One who has the power and victory before any battle has ever been fought. You can stand without fear for He is with you. As you stand in Him, you will be trained expertly with the weapons of spiritual warfare. No one else can wield the weapons because they are not worthy. Because He is worthy of all praise, it is His privilege to dispense these to those who will use them for His glory.

By yourself, you can do nothing. However, the strength and ability that God brings to you, that He equips you with in the secret place, allows you to accomplish great and mighty exploits. You are able to truly go beyond yourself and war in The Spirit where He has placed every weapon in your hands, trained you how to use them, and given the strength and ability to wield them expertly in every battle. The victory is already The Lord's, therefore you can walk forth victoriously in every area!!

CONCLUSION

The strength and might of a warrior is not what is placed in his hands, but who has trained him and what he has learned. A true warrior will use what is at hand and the skill of the training to be as obedient as possible.

It is time for you to use whatever is at hand, to pick up and destroy the enemy. Rise up, move forward, and advance The Kingdom with what has been given you at this moment. Continuously be built up and continually hone the weapon that you have, preparing for the upgrade that is coming your way.

The arming of a warrior is the attitude, mindset, heart to advance, taking of ground, and willingness to do whatever is asked of him because The Commander has spoken. This is the heart of a warrior, "Here I am send me". I will go because the mission needs someone to complete it.

The Warrior is armed with vision from The Almighty, the download of destiny from The King, the mindset of The Master, and a pure heart's desire to please The Commander by advancing The Kingdom!

To become a warrior, you must be stripped of worldly mindsets and mentalities and built up in desires of The King and Master. The destiny and legacy of The Kingdom is something bigger than yourself. This is something that you have to come to understand. Every true warrior thrives knowing it is not about him, but about the greater good of the mission. Once this is achieved, no excuse, obstacle, trouble, trial, or problem in this world will hold you back from overcoming and pressing forward into all that you have been created for (*Rom 8:31-39*). This is how warriors are made!

The best warrior is the one who has blood in the battle. The one who is there because he has been drafted or for short term personal gain, will cut and run at the first sign of defeat.

In the movie The Patriot, Mel Gibson's character is a part of an army that is untested in open field combat. They have come to fight against the well-trained British army. Gibson has only joined the Continentals because his son was brutally murdered by a British commanding officer. On the field, the continentals resolve is wavering, and they are beginning to retreat in front of the British. Gibson lays aside his person-

al agenda and grabs a flag racing to the front line. As he runs, he yells, "no retreat!"

Here he acts as a warrior because he has blood in the game. He has an investment in defeating the enemy. He does not even need a physical weapon to inspire his fellow fighters not to run but to stand firm. His inspiration leads not only to a strengthened resolve but the defeat and retreat of the enemy. As a warrior, this must be your resolve: **"No retreat!!!" "Not one inch!!!"**

True, raw grit is what defines the greatest warriors. To never give up, never back down, and never surrender is the heart of the warrior. Even if every weapon is stripped or warring implement lost, the drive to take out the enemy will keep the warrior going. He will use whatever he has at hand with skill and ingenuity to advance his destiny's cause. This is what he lives for. The Warrior is not afraid to give up his life for the greater good. But neither will he be taken out easily.

Every warrior will fight to the last breath, inflicting as much damage as can be done on the enemy. Fighting with the knowledge that those who come after him will benefit from the strength, bravery, and raw grit that comes from knowing and advancing the plans and purposes of the Kingdom.

Where does this warrior mindset come from? The more you spend time with the Lord of Angel Armies, the more you will discover your sonship in His presence. The more your specific plan, purpose, and destiny is revealed; the harder you will fight for the advancement of The Kingdom.

It is time to step up and step out into your calling and purpose as a warrior and carry out the destiny and orders you have been given. This desire must not come from plans for personal gain, but a desire to please The King of Kings that can only come from time spent with Him in The Presence!!!

CHAPTER 6
SLAYING GIANTS

"Every giant will fall,
The mountains will move
Every chain of the past,
You've broken in two
Over fear, over lies,
We're singing the truth
That nothing is impossible with You"
(*Every Giant Will Fall* by Rend Collective)

FOR ALL THOSE who desire to know their God, and be strong, they must do great exploits (*Dan 11:32*). Great destiny and great legacy breeds great adversaries. The enemy will not sit back and do nothing waiting for you to advance. Great opposition has already taken place, and veritable giants have been placed in the way of you walking into the promised land God has for you. The gates of hell have set themselves up in the path of your destiny that The Kingdom might be hindered from the exponential growth that will take place in and through you. No matter the shape, size, or manifestation of this evil, **these giants must be slain for you to enter into the fullness of The Kingdom.**

Every great warrior must battle and overcome a great enemy. **True greatness is not discovered in the training, but in the proving ground.** You have been armed not to become some Olympic trophy winner, but to overcome, destroy, and decimate every adversary that would raise its head to hinder The Kingdom. Giants cannot be pushed out, but must be beheaded and completely eradicated. If the thorns are not uprooted, they will become a thorn in your side not only for you, but also for those who will come after you. **True warriors will destroy the enemy now rather than face him again later in life.**

> *"But if you do not drive out the inhabitants of the land from before you, then those you let remain of them will be like pricks in your eyes and like thorns in your sides, and they will attack you in the land in which you live."*
> ***Numbers 33:55***

Heads will roll in the warriors camp. **Warriors fight to overcome, conquer, and win the war.** This can never be done if your enemy is left alive to regroup and return. Every battle must be fought like it is the most important one you will ever face.

> *"For the Lord has driven out great and mighty nations from before you; and as for you, no man has been able to stand [in opposition] before you to this day. One of your men puts to flight a thousand, for the Lord your God is He who is fighting for you, just as He promised you. So be very careful and watchful of yourselves to love the Lord your God...; ...not one word of all the good words which the Lord your God has promised concerning you has failed..."*
> ***Joshua 23:9-11, 14***

For those who walk in The Way, your enemies are the adversaries of The Lord. You are on His side, and He will fight for you. As a warrior, your primary responsibility is to walk with God and love Him with all your heart. In this way, you will conquer every enemy because your ally is greater than anything that would ever raise its head against you. God will not fail you! He is faithful to His promise!

There are many enemies that will come against you. Here are some of the most common giants that you have been empowered to overcome:

- Fear
- Pride
- Rebellion
- Unbelief
- Religion
- Selfishness
- Lust of flesh
- Insecurity/Lack of Identity

The giant of fear may be the most common opponent to the plans and purposes of The Lord. **The enemy wants you to back down before you even try.** This happened with the people of Israel when they got to the Promised Land. This happened with Goliath who stood against the armies of Israel. This happened with every Judge that was awakened to the promise of God and empowered to be a deliverer of the people. Even Pharaoh is an example of this, he stood in opposition to Moses and the freeing of the people.

Too often, people of God can get tired of the battle and begin to settle into a land filled with giants. They begin to live and cohabit with the enemy as God never intended. Cohabiting too long will lead to intermarrying and a blurring of the holiness that is designed for God's people. **We are designed to be set apart warriors not camouflaged couch potatoes.** Warriors do not blend in with the unrighteousness around them. The holiness of God's people must never be tainted with the ways of the world. Even the mighty Samson began to flirt with the Philistines that were the mortal enemies of the Israelites. Samson could have been a mighty warrior, but he never did overcome the giant of the lust of the flesh.

The giants of the land will cause you to step into the greatness of the destiny God has created for you. Never reject the plan and purpose of The Lord because of the giants that stand in the way. **How you handle** the giants in front of you will determine what kind of warrior you will become.

> *"The Lord said to Joshua, 'See, I have given Jericho into your hand, with its king and the mighty warriors'."*
> *Joshua 6:2*

God has already given you everything you need to overcome even the mighty enemy and false rulers of the Promised Land. The only reason they are there is to oppose you. If you were not a threat, they would never be set up in your way. The true grit to overcome every obstacle and eradicate every enemy in the way of your destiny calling will cause you to slay veritable giants and false rulers in the land. You must step up and step into all that God has designed for you!

Never settle for second best by living in a land filled with giants! Eliminate every enemy and step up into The Promise of The Kingdom!

I recently read a book about the smallest man to ever join the special forces. He was under the minimum height and weight requirements to even be considered, but this did not stop him. You see, to him, everyone was a giant. He faced giants daily and did not allow other people's view of his size to slacken his resolve or determination. He would take a beating but would get up and keep on going. He was able to carry as much weight as the largest person on his team.

His resolve never slackened at the size of the mission, or the fear that was his constant companion. When his men were trapped behind enemy lines with no way of escape, he took it upon himself to get to them and bring them back. The giants in his way did not stand a chance because if he could not defeat them head on, he would back up, take a running start, and take out their legs. He did whatever necessary to defeat any enemy that stood in his way, no matter how big or impossible the foe may seem. He proved himself to his team and opponents alike and overcame, despite the physical disadvantages, even earning several meritorious awards for his service including the silver star. (*Giant Killer* by David Yuzuk)

What about you? What is your resolve? What will be your determination? Size or maturity in The Spirit does not matter as much as your willingness and resolution to overcome.

You probably know the story of David and Goliath, but let me add another thought. David was young, smaller in stature than Goliath and far less trained. He did not have war gear, experience, or anyone that believed in him. When he went to battle, he took his sling and staff. On the way he picked up five stones. Many people will say he did this because he knew Goliath had four brothers. I doubt this. **David was not up to date on the family history of this giant.** He did not need to be. **He was current with his relationship with the Lord.** Later, David says *"Even though I walk through the valley of the shadow of death, I will fear no evil... for your rod and staff comfort me"* (**Psalm 23:4**). The staff that David took was a symbol that God was with him. It is easy to stand back far removed from the battle of David and say, he knew he would win with one stone and took four others for his brothers and all kinds of things.

What if David were like you and I?

Alone, inexperienced. Walking through the wilderness with sheep, even after being anointed as king in the secret place. All David had was what he had gained in spending time with The Lord. He knew God was with Him. He knew God had delivered him from smaller foes. He knew this giant stood in the way of the Promised Land of God's people.

This giant had to fall one way or the other. David felt that since God was with him, he would be helped to defeat the enemy. I believe he took five stones because that is all he could carry. I think he took his staff because he was ready to go close quarters combat with a battle-hardened giant if that is what was required of him. He knew, even if no one else did, it was the king's job to destroy the giants that would arise in the land. He was anointed, God was with him, and **he was willing to die being obedient to God rather than live in a land ruled by giants.**

I believe this is what drove David into "*the valley of the shadow of death*," God was with Him, and God told Him to go. I am not even so sure he knew he would survive the encounter. **Raw obedience to walk in The Wilderness Way had taught him that this was the only way forward.**

When the stone knocked Goliath unconscious, you notice that David did not start his celebration at once. He immediately ran to where the giant had fallen, took the sword and cut off his head. Goliath was not dead until his head was separated from his shoulders. David did not hesitate, but moved to completely remove any chance of the enemy rising again.

The head of the giant became the banner that rallied the fearful men of Israel to pursue the rest of the enemy. **David, the anointed king, stepped into his God-given destiny the very moment he chose raw obedience and eradication of the enemy of God's people.**

There is a saying about giants, "The bigger they are, the harder they fall." This is how you should look at the opposition in your way. No matter what hindrance is in the way of you walking into your God-given destiny, it must be brought down. It may take time, strategy, or uncommon tactics to take it down, but giants were never made to stand. They were made to be your bread. The giant was made for you to feast upon the victory of his defeat and stretch you to grow and overcome every weakness that would hold you back.

> "*Only do not rebel against the Lord, nor fear the people of the land, for they are our bread; their protection has departed from them, and the Lord is with us. Do not fear them.*"
> **Numbers 14:9** (NKJV)

Jesus said, "*Man cannot live on bread alone, but every word that proceeds from the mouth of God*" (**Matt 4:4** NKJV). Live in obedience to The Word of God, and this will cause you to feast upon the bodies of fallen giants. The wilderness can be hard, discouraging, and even depressing in some cases, but **the wilderness is the training grounds to prepare** you to radically overcome every giant that would raise its head to oppose you.

Never let fear or intimidation cause you to remain in the wilderness training time when you have been called out to advance in position and rank. It is time to receive the reward of defeated devils and feast upon the greatness of the promises revealed.

You were never brought into the wilderness to starve or die. You were led here to learn the necessity of being in The Presence and receiving the daily bread, The very Word of God. From this place, you will be led to mature from bread to meat.

> *"So the people spoke against God and against Moses, "Why have you brought us out of Egypt to die in the wilderness? For there is no bread, nor is there any water, and we loathe this miserable food."*
> *Numbers 21:5*

The Israelites in the desert grew tired of the daily bread quickly. They craved meat to eat, but they had no teeth, no spiritual grit that would cause them to dig in and rally to victory over the giants. This is the real reason they did not enter the Promised Land. They did not trust The Lord to lead them to victory. He had performed mighty signs and wonders to deliver them from slavery. Often the people of God can remain in this place of freedom from death and deliverance from sin, but become bored with the bread.

You were never meant to live on just bread. It is not enough to survive, but you have been called to thrive and grow in Christ. You can never become more than a conqueror if you never face a giant. The path out of the wilderness into the Promised Land is through the valley of the shadow of death. There will be evil, there will be giants, but there is a table of feasting set for those who are able to overcome the opposition of the enemy.

You must move from the manna of daily bread, to the bodies of giants for daily sustenance. Just like David, just like Joshua, you bring the rod of God's presence with you. You must continue to receive and live upon the daily bread of divine encounters with Him, but you also must level up by overcoming each and every giant that is revealed.

Each giant has a unique weapon that will aid in slaying the next enemy that will arise. The slaying of Goliath caused a new giant to arise for David, jealous Saul. When David was on the run from Saul, he took Goliath's sword, because there was none like it. Not only was this the weapon that brought to remembrance David's past victory, it was what he needed to level up into being the leader of outcasts and rebels and bring them into transformation. This is how they became David's mighty men.

The jealousy, anger and fear of man that defeated Saul were defeated when David took the water jug and spear from a sleeping giant. David placed the honor of a king on a man that did not deserve to live. He did not overcome evil with evil but overcame jealousy, anger, and the counsel of man to defeat a giant in his own heart. Because of this, David goes from victory to victory even in the wilderness, and God Himself prepares the way for David to become king.

It is time for you to move from milk to meat, from manna to defeated giants!

Dragons need slaying! Wild beasts need to be destroyed so they can no longer wreak havoc on the Kingdom. Only the bravest would go out to face such mighty beasts. The reward for the conquest of such foes is the best The Kingdom has to offer. But for the true warrior, the reward of one conquest will be the even greater one that follows. The Kingdom must be rid of every vile creature that would hurt the innocent and prey on the weak.

> *"... you have become dull and sluggish in [your spiritual] hearing and disinclined to listen.... you have come to be continually in need of milk, not solid food. For everyone who lives on milk is [doctrinally*

inexperienced and] unskilled in the word of righteousness, since he is a spiritual infant. But solid food is for the [spiritually] mature, whose senses are trained by practice to distinguish between what is morally good and what is evil."
Hebrews 5:11-14

Could it be that the people of God grew restless in the wilderness because they were never able to overcome the giants placed in front of them?

They were tired of pure milk but had chosen to live with the mediocre giants of comfort and complacency. They were never able to overcome these giants so they had no spiritual meat.

While in the wilderness the people had to trust the daily manna, encounter with God, to keep them sustained. As you enter The Promise, you must learn to be fed by the daily defeat of giants and the "bread" that comes from these overcoming victories.

"'Give us this day our daily bread...
And do not lead us into temptation, but deliver us from evil.'"
Matthew 6:11,13

As you advance into maturity, there are at least two levels of advancement noted in these verses:

- Deliver us from evil

Stage one is to not let evil overcome your camp where you are. Deliver me from the attack of the enemy and keep me from every scheme.

Stage two is to not let evil overcome you as you advance into the enemy's territory. The attack of the evil one will come as you step forward into the Promised Land. However, you will be set free from being overwhelmed by remaining in The Promise.

For both of these stages, the importance of completely decimating the enemy is seen. He must be defeated and never rise again to oppose you or future generations. The enemy cannot overcome you as you rise in victory and proceed to overcoming. To advance The Kingdom, you must destroy every strongman that would stand in the way.

- *Give us this day our daily bread*

Stage one is manna, the daily Word of God continually sustaining you. As you remain in this place constantly, you will progress to stage two. Stage two is victory over giants in the Promised Land. The manna of heaven will lead to feasting on the defeated enemy. Slain giants are the sustenance of the mature and will lead to greater levels of authority and responsibility. If you are faithful with a little, you will be given more.

In the wilderness you learn to survive, in the Promised Land you learn how to keep each other progressing and thriving while continually advancing and taking ground.

Overcoming the giants and advancing into The Promised Land is much like leveling up in a video game, or working your way up from the bottom in a competition. As you defeat each opponent, you gain a skill, knowledge, advantage or tactic that is necessary to overcome in the daily walk of life.

Remembering back to most games, you literally could not defeat certain bosses until you found that treasure. You could not access entire worlds until the boss was defeated. In much the same way, the "momentary light affliction" or intense combat training (depending on which side of the battle you are in) gives you exactly what you need not only to slay the giant, but to walk at a new level and in a new place with The Lord. The slain giants, the skills, weapons, and wisdom that you gained as you sought the Lord to overcome, will become your sustenance. This will be your strength and vitality walking every day into the Promised Land that God has for you.

The strength of the giant should only confirm the strength that God has placed within you to overcome it. It may take some time, training, and unique tactics or weapons, but **you were created to enter the promised destiny.**

You are an overcomer!

Nothing can stand in your way!

Set your heart to seek The Lord and follow Him completely and totally. Wherever you may be in your walk with The Lord, He will help you to overcome any and every giant that would raise its head to combat The Kingdom. God's Kingdom is ever-increasing and eternally advancing. This is why every giant must be slain. So they do not hinder you, or the generations that will come after you, from receiving the fullness of the inheritance.

The giants control the enemy strongholds that have been set up to occupy the mountains (the high places). The weakness of humanity has given these places over to false masters. In the absence of the power of the people of God, giants have arisen and grown strong.

By inactivity and disobedience, the people of God have given them the right and authority to rule in their promised land. **This can no longer be the case.** You cannot give away the power and authority that has been given to you by Jesus' victory. You cannot let these weapons lay dormant because of complacency, disobedience, or fear. **It is time for you to arise and take up the weapon of sonship that has been given to you.** The value of this implementation is priceless because it was paid for by the blood of Jesus, and you cannot waste your life or energy on things of this world any longer. **Arise and slay the giants that stand in the way of you receiving the fullness of your inheritance!!!**

The giants must be beheaded for the people of God to lay claim to their rightful inheritance. **You cannot allow these things to live in any capacity.** They must be destroyed and the next generation must be trained to overcome these giants as well. A giant is easier to destroy before it is fully grown. **You must give no foothold to the enemy, "Not one inch!!!"**

When the people of Israel came to their promised land, they sent leaders as spies into the land to bring back news. This is what happened.

> *"Now they departed and came back to Moses and Aaron and all the congregation of the children of Israel in the Wilderness of Paran, at Kadesh; they brought back word to them and to all the congregation, and showed them the fruit of the land."*
> **Numbers 13:25** (NKJV)

The people in the wilderness were waiting for the good word of the Lord. In unison, the spies brought back word that the Promised Land was good and full of fruit. This was the time for them to move forward and possess the land. However, the spies went from focusing on the promise of God, to be with them and give them this good land, to personal thoughts, ideas, and fears.

> *"Nevertheless the people who dwell in the land are strong; the cities are fortified and very large; moreover we saw the descendants of Anak there."*
> **Numbers 13:28** (NKJV)

As a warrior called to slay giants and walk in the good things of the Lord, when you speak the word of God, you are an encouragement to everyone around you. This bread that you receive from heaven should be shared. However, when you begin to speak fear and doubt and lead people away from the word and promise of the Lord, you are robbing them of the **Promised Land** and putting them on the path to more wilderness wandering or a return to the bondage they have been freed from. **You must always speak hope and faith as a son,** not fear and doubt as a slave.

> *"Then Caleb quieted the people before Moses, and said, 'Let us go up at once and take possession, for we are well able to overcome it.'"*
> **Numbers 13:30** (NKJV)

Caleb was a son, a warrior, one who heard The Word of The Lord and spoke it for all to hear. He did not care that he was in the minority among men because he was aligning himself with The Word of God. Walking in the way of The Lord, in communion with Him and His Word, you will enter The Promised Land no matter what the circumstance around you or who may stand against you.

> *"But the men who had gone up with him said, 'We are not able to go up against the people, for they are stronger than we.' And they gave the children of Israel a bad report of the land which they had spied out, saying, 'The land through which we have gone as spies is a land that devours its inhabitants, and all the people whom we saw in it are men of great stature. There we saw the giants (the descendants of Anak came from the giants); and we were like grasshoppers in our own sight, and so we were in their sight.'"*
> *Numbers 13:31-33* (NKJV)

In this case, as so happens even today, fear masqueraded as wisdom. They went from speaking their personal fears to full on demonic influence of the people. They even went from speaking the truth about the goodness of the land to saying this land devours its inhabitants. They spoke from the place of captivity in the mind, saying "they will squash us like bugs and eat us".

> *"And all the children of Israel complained against Moses and Aaron, and the whole congregation said to them, 'If only we had died in the land of Egypt! Or if only we had died in this wilderness! Why has the Lord brought us to this land to fall by the sword, that our wives and children should become victims? Would it not be better for us to return to Egypt?'"*
> *Numbers 14:2-3* (NKJV)

Fear began to run rampant and caused the people to move from the place of faith and hope that God was with them to lead them into the Promised Land, to desiring the slavery, captivity, and death that they continually complained about. Everything they had ever dreamed of lay before them, and they chose to overlook the power of God that freed them and fed them. This led them to partner with the fear of the ene-my, and continue in the wilderness, waiting for another generation to arise.

> *"But Joshua the son of Nun and Caleb the son of Jephunneh, who were among those who had spied out the land, tore their clothes; and they spoke to all the congregation of the children of Israel, saying: 'The land we passed through to spy out is an exceedingly good land. If the Lord delights in us, then He will bring us into this land and give it to us, 'a land which flows with milk and honey.' Only do not rebel against the Lord, nor fear the people of the land, for they are our bread; their protection has departed from them, and the Lord is with us. Do not fear them.'"*
> ***Numbers 14:7-9*** (NKJV)

Two men stood up and began to speak the truth of the land and of the power of God. Even the giants would be consumed because the land was the good, promised land that God said He would bring them into. Interestingly, you do not see Moses saying anything. I do not know if he was waiting to see what happened or sitting back passively.

Was he so frustrated with the people that he would not speak to the circumstance?

It seems that he abdicated his place of leadership and essentially said "Let the people decide what they want to do." If this was the case, another lesson to learn is to **never be passive about The Word of The Lord.** Moses never entered the Promised Land.

Was the real decision made here because he did not stand and speak the Word of the Lord as at other times?

Had he chosen to walk into the Promised Land by himself and leave the people wandering if God would let him?

It would seem that Joshua and Caleb were more influential and righteous at this time than Moses. Whether this was a test or a failure in leadership, Joshua and Caleb make the decision at this moment that will cause them to rise to leadership in maturity and authority. The spiritual sons arose, spoke The Word of The Lord, and radically stood against the crowd on the Lord's side.

This was their immediate reward:

> "And all the congregation said to stone them with stones. Now the glory of the Lord appeared in the tabernacle of meeting before all the children of Israel."
> **Numbers 14:10** (NKJV)

The people were ready to stone those in opposition to what they wanted to do. Speaking The Truth does not make you a lot of friends. However, it is better to be a son of God and an enemy of the world than to partner with worldly mindsets. **God is the one who will defeat every giant through your hands of obedience.** The world will lead you to obscurity and destruction. Not one of the other spies was even named; but here, and later before the next generation, Joshua and Caleb are commended by God. He manifests His presence and speaks. Even if no one will side with Joshua and Caleb, God Himself does.

Giants will only be defeated when we place ourselves in complete alignment with The Lord.

> "Then David said to the Philistine, 'You come to me with a sword, with a spear, and with a javelin. But I come to you in the name of the Lord of hosts, the God of the armies of Israel, whom you have defied. This day the Lord will deliver you into my hand, and I will strike you and take your head from you... that all the earth may know that there is a God in Israel...
> The battle is the Lord's, and He will give you into our hands.'"
> **1 Samuel 17:45-46** (NKJV)

David knew that the physical armor or weapon in his hands was not the greatest tool to overcome the enemy. He had come to realize that the way he positioned himself would set him up for victory or defeat. Goliath had spent forty days spewing his poison and fear to infuse the people of God with deceit. If he could cause them to agree with what their eyes saw, he would not even have to raise his spear. In fact, the only thing he had to raise for the last five weeks was his voice.

Now, this young, inexperienced boy was coming against the demonic structure that Goliath had built. No one had dared oppose the monument of fear that had been built until this shepherd came to the battle. David was not looking with his physical eyes to the size and difficulty of the battle, he was placing himself directly in the path of victory. The giant was standing in the way of the future king's kingdom. He had been anointed to rule this area of land, and now he was being tested if he would stand up to the enemy.

David was not all talk. He truly believed that God was with Him and that he would overcome every obstacle in opposition to the call of God on his life. **His actions proved what he believed.**

> *"So it was, when the Philistine arose and came and drew near to meet David, that David hurried and ran toward the army to meet the Philistine."*
> *1 Samuel 17:48* (NKJV)

David the shepherd, who was inferior in size, weaponry, and experience, ran toward the enemy. He could not wait for the enemy to prepare for the attack, he knew that active, accelerating advancement is the plan of The Lord. Not only was he running to face the giant, he was advancing toward the enemy army which hopelessly outnumbered him. I do not think David gets enough credit for the position he took with The Advancing, Almighty God.

> *"Then David put his hand in his bag and took out a stone; and he slung it and struck the Philistine in his forehead, so that the stone sank into his forehead, and he fell on his face to the earth. So David prevailed over the Philistine with a sling and a stone, and struck the Philistine and killed him. But there was no sword in the hand*

of David. Therefore David ran and stood over the Philistine, took his sword and drew it out of its sheath and killed him, and cut off his head with it. And when the Philistines saw that their champion was dead, they fled."
1 Samuel 17:50-51 (NKJV)

David recognized The Almighty would empower him to defeat this giant. Even though the enemy had fallen, David could not allow this enemy to ever rise again. For this reason, he took the very weapon of the enemy and removed all doubt that this enemy was completely destroyed. The weapon of fear was defeated, and the enemy army now fled in fear at the power of God on display. This boy had easily overcome their very best, and they saw the determination in his eyes to come for them next. No enemy even tried to stand up to David who had placed himself in the position of son and king in the path of victory into the Promised Land.

This was not David's first victory over the enemy, and it would not be the last. However, the precept was established for him, all the people, and for you. The Almighty has power over every enemy, and you must stand with Him. **No matter the enemy, whatever the circumstances, walking in The Presence of The Almighty will lead you into all victory!!!**

Giant killers will raise up other giant killers. David, who defeated the giant Goliath, began to be hunted by Saul. He lived in the wilderness, and outcasts were drawn to him. From these worthless men, later came the Mighty Men of David that were known for defeating giants and doing great exploits. David was not only able to defeat his own giants, he began to raise men who were able to do the same, and this is who he ran with for the rest of his life.

"Then Ishbi-Benob, who was one of the sons of the giant, the weight of whose bronze spear was three hundred shekels, who was bearing a new sword, thought he could kill David. But Abishai the son of Zeruiah came to his aid, and struck the Philistine and killed him..."

2 Samuel 21:16-17 (NKJV)

The son of the giant was killed by the "son" of the warrior. No one remembers Abishai's name, but without him there would be no David. Your decisions now, to slay giants and raise up a generation of giant killers, will save you strife, and maybe your life, later on.

> *"Then Sibbechai the Hushathite killed Saph, who was one of the sons of the giant."*
> *2 Samuel 21:18* (NKJV)

Who can even pronounce the name of this guy let alone remember it? But here, almost as a postscript, he is slaying one of the other sons of Goliath. This was not an impressive or mighty work, it was day to day life for the giant killers.

> *"Again there was war at Gob with the Philistines, where Elhanan the son of Jaare-Oregim the Bethlehemite killed the brother of Goliath the Gittite, the shaft of whose spear was like a weaver's beam."*
> *2 Samuel 21:19* (NKJV)

Here is another footnote in history. The greatness of killing giants had become commonplace in this troop. I can almost hear them saying, "Yeah, Elhanan bagged another big one, it's what we do."

> *"Yet again there was war at Gath, where there was a man of great stature, who had six fingers on each hand and six toes on each foot, twenty-four in number; and he also was born to the giant. So when he defied Israel, Jonathan the son of Shimea, David's brother, killed him. These four were born to the giant in Gath, and fell by the hand of David and by the hand of his servants."*
> *2 Samuel 21:20-22* (NKJV)

This time, David's nephew slays a strange one. His relation to David may have caused him to be bold and continue the exploits of his uncle. However, it was the community of giant slayers around him that encouraged him to keep on slaying giants and pressing into the promised land no matter the size or strangeness of those that stood in the way. David and his men literally destroy all of the giants in the land. After this, there are no more physical giants mentioned. Then the enemies of Israel are because of sheer numbers.

Are there still giants today? Yes, but the spiritual giants are what you have to overcome. **You must eradicate every spiritual giant that stands in the way of you entering into your destiny whatever the strength or size of the enemy and his force.**

> "*Benaiah the son of Jehoiada, the son of a courageous man of Kabzeel who had done great things, killed the two sons of Ariel of Moab...*"
> *1 Chronicles 11:22* (NKJV)

What is Legacy? Benaiah was the son of a courageous man. Jehoida's name is barely mentioned, but he named his son and raised him as a warrior. He did not focus on only what he could do in his own time period, or he would have been completely forgotten. He instilled the best of what he had and helped his son to step into his full role and let him become who he was called to be. Because of this, Benaiah becomes one of the most well known warriors of David. **He was not the most skilled or advanced, but he had the legacy of greatness ingrained within him.** It was not only who he was, but it helped him to pass this on to everyone around him.

He was not consumed by fear, but knew the strength and power of God to overcome every enemy. Because of this he killed two lion-like men of Moab. The verse continues:

> "*...Also he went down and killed a lion in a pit on a snowy day.*" *1 Chronicles 11:22* (NKJV)

His father had trained him not to accept passivity in any form, but to be continuously active in his calling. **No enemy, man or beast, was al-**

lowed in his land to steal, kill, and destroy. He would not permit cattle, children, or other warriors to be wounded or killed because he let an enemy live in his land. The climate and location of the enemy did not stop Benaiah from going and completely destroying this monster. **He could not allow anything around him to live that would consume his destiny or legacy.**

> *"He killed an Egyptian also, a man of great stature, five cubits tall. In the Egyptian's hand was a spear like a weaver's beam, and Benaiah went down to him with [only] a staff (rod) and grabbed the spear from the Egyptian's hand and killed him with his own spear."*
> *1 Chronicles 11:23* (AMP)

The legacy of the warrior was continued as he came upon a pagan foreigner that was a giant. This giant was over seven and a half feet tall and apparently was a well-trained enemy. At the time, Benaiah did not have the most suitable weapon for destroying giants, but he had a staff (representation of God being with him). **He used what he had to overcome the enemy and gained a new weapon to deal with the enemy once and for all.** I wonder if this spear became his weapon of choice as he continued on in his great giant-killing exploits.

> *"Benaiah the son of Jehoiada did these things, and had a name as well as the three mighty men. He was honored among the thirty, but he did not attain to [the rank of] the [first] three. David appointed him over his bodyguard."*
> *1 Chronicles 11:24-25* (AMP)

Benaiah was not the greatest, best or most honored, but he was a giant slayer. **He did not allow the enemy to get a foothold in his inheritance. He was not intimidated by the size or tactics of the enemy.** His father had taught him to slay giants and that is what he would do for his entire life.

David surrounded himself with mighty men, but he appointed Benaiah over his personal bodyguards. *Why?*

David wanted to surround himself with the people who would encourage and push him to greatness (iron sharpening iron *Psalm 27:17*).

Later on, Benaiah would become the commander of the army. This was not because he was the best warrior. **Because of the importance he placed on actively living with no compromise, not allowing the enemy to have one inch of the inheritance, and the value and legacy of training up the next warrior generation, he was seen as the best person to pass on this mentality to an entire company of next-generation warriors that they might become giant slayers themselves.** As this new company advanced, they would also have the ability to overcome every enemy and multiply the victory from generation to generation as true legacy was built.

Benaiah means, "Son of God, built (structurally of stone) by God." An important thing that Jehoida had done in the training and raising of his giant-killing, legacy-building son was naming him. **It is the responsibility of a good father and leader to name and call out of your sons their divine destiny.** Jehoida knew that to become the giant killer, his son must first come to know the strength and power of God. Being built up in Him would help Benaiah to become and sustain the nature of giant-slayer and eventually become the commander of the people of God.

The giants that you face now are not the physical giants of the past. These are giants of sin, destruction and death that would seek to distract, diminish, and destroy the people of God in any way possible. The giants serve the enemy who will steal, kill, and destroy as much as you allow him. Whether it comes as an overt attack or they hide in the shadows manipulating and sabotaging lives, destinies, and legacies; these giants will continually do whatever they can to rob you of your eternal heavenly purpose. This is why they must be completely destroyed!!!

How do you slay the spiritual giants and destroy every dark demon?
Paul has some words of wisdom for you to start your study:

"For though we walk in the flesh, we do not war according to the flesh. For the weapons of our warfare are not carnal..."
2 Corinthians 10:3-4 (NKJV)

As was discussed in the previous chapter, your weapons to defeat these giants are not physical. Though it might be easier to see in the physical and fight with a sword or spear, this is not what will destroy the giants lurking at the edge of the Promised Land.

The verse continues -
"...They are mighty in God for":

- pulling down strongholds

What is a stronghold, but a place ruled by a giant. Because of thoughts, beliefs, and actions coinciding with these false beliefs, he has gained a strong hold in the life of the individual. **These can only be rooted out by identifying the lie or false belief, repenting of the sin of siding with the enemy, and replacing it with The Truth of The Word that applies in the situation.** Doing this will not only ensure the removal of the stronghold, but will destroy the hold of the giant and decapitate him so he will not return at a later time of weakness.

- casting down arguments

The giants will try to lure you to begin to walk in unbelief. They will raise disagreements with God's Word through situations, circumstances, and people that seem to challenge with God's Word, purpose, and destiny. You must never join yourself to any word that contradicts God's Word because this empowers the giant with agreement. **Stand firm on the promises of God.** When you agree with Him, no enemy can stand against you because the battle becomes His. You must begin to learn how to cast down these words that do not line up with the plans, purpose, or character of God and not even let your thoughts dwell on these deceptions.

- casting down every high thing that exalts itself against the knowledge of God,

Another major giant that wants to consume you is pride. This enemy will cause you to begin to look at yourself and lift yourself higher than God. Few people would see how they do this, but when you begin to choose your own way instead of God's way, exalt your experience and opinion above what God has revealed in His Word, or live in the way that pleases your flesh no matter the consequences, you have been overtaken by the giant of pride.

Pride will cause the wisdom of the world and a personal opinion to take precedence over what God has spoken. No matter what the source of such things, if it is not consistent with what God has spoken, it is a high thing that must be cast down. **The Word of The Lord must be exalted above every other thing in your life no matter what you may see in the flesh.** The King's standard is always raised higher than your own. His way is the only way into the Promised Land.

- bringing every thought into captivity to the obedience of Christ

Imagination is a great gift of God that causes you to dream and realize things that have never existed before. Technologies and inventions come from godly creative imagination and have benefited the entire human race. As with every gift of God, the enemy would seek to hijack and pervert this grace. This is why you are commanded to bring every thought under Kingdom rule. Doubts, fears, and unbelief will arise as a mere thought or question. When the enemy tempts Eve in the garden and later Jesus in the wilderness, you see that he comes not in direct opposition, but with supposedly harmless questions. "Did God really say?" "If you are...". **Small thoughts can quickly become giants**

that hijack destinies if you dwell on them and let them grow. Like a splinter, they must be quickly removed and thrown out before they fester and begin to influence other thoughts, beliefs, and actions.

- punishing all disobedience when your obedience is fulfilled.

No matter what you say or do, you can never cause someone else to walk in The Wilderness Way. You can influence or counsel other people, but they must make their own decision. In your own life, you must learn to recognize the difference between obedience and disobedience. You must increasingly continue walking in obedience, and disobedience must be recognized and repented of quickly. **The more you see and recognize areas that are out of line with the will of God and bring them into Kingdom agreement, the more rapidly you will return to full obedience and alignment with The Kingdom.**

You are called to operate outside yourself and your abilities. You might be able to take on a battle in the natural, but there is a larger, more important fight taking place. People are not your enemy no matter how they may treat you or what they will say about you. You must ascend to where the real confrontation is taking place.

> **Ephesians 6:12** *"For we do not wrestle against flesh and blood, but against:*

- *principalities,*
- *powers*

- *rulers of the darkness of this age*
- *spiritual hosts of wickedness in the heavenly places"*

All of these things are able to influence more than just a single person. However, people are used as weapons to build or destroy one Kingdom or the other. When you yield yourself to The Master and allow Him to use you in the greatest way possible, by complete obedience and unyielding faith, you will begin not just to slay giants but dismantle the works of the enemy in every area. It will probably take more than just one or two days, but destroying every work of darkness and building The Kingdom is worth the time, energy, and effort. **He is worthy to receive the reward of His suffering!!!**

In fact, you have already been given this victory over every evil power. You have the power, might, and ability as you come into unity with The Victorious, Risen Lord!!!

> *"...having nailed it to the cross. Having disarmed principalities and powers, He made a public spectacle of them, triumphing over them in it." Colossians 2:14-15* (NKJV)

Triumph and victory are yours to take hold of as you take hold of Christ. Hell, death, and the grave have been defeated and openly displayed as fallen. Now is the time to arise and step fully into your role as more than a conqueror.

Victorious warriors arise!!! Do not allow a defeated enemy to sabotage any more of the land that is no longer his. The giants must be slain never to rise again, and the generations must be trained to walk in this victory that you have already been given.

There is a tendency to give the world too much credit. The world is empowered by giving your attention and affection to the things it produces. Yielding to the idols of entertainment and complacency that comes from the lullaby that is being sweetly played for the masses, can cause even mighty warriors to take a knee or close their eyes for a moment or two. **Righteousness must spring forth and destroy every evil influence that entices you and seeks to capture your heart.** You are a citizen of The Kingdom and a redeemed creation.

> *"For all that is in the world—*
> *the lust of the flesh,*
> *the lust of the eyes, and*
> *the pride of life—*

is not of the Father but is of the world. And the world is passing away, and the lust of it; but he who does the will of God abides forever." 1 John 2:16-17 (NKJV)

You are not one of these things that waste away and are destroyed. You are an eternal being designed to worship The Creator of all things. You must never love a lesser, perishing, enemy-inspired idol. You must look to The One at whose name every knee will bow, and every tongue confess, "Jesus, You are Lord!!!"

Victory has already been given, but it must be taken a hold of. If you do not receive and walk in this gift, you will sink into the mire of this world. No more wasted lives! No more collateral damage! Not one inch yielded to a fallen, defeated enemy. He has already lost the battle in the heavens. You must not allow him to occupy any area on the earth that you have been given dominion over. Power and authority is within your grasp. **Take hold of what you have been given and advance The Kingdom in every area. Whatever you have to give up, no matter the cost or sacrifice, The Kingdom is worth far more!!!** Declare this to the atmosphere, "*I will be joined with the Victorious One and truly become more than a conqueror but a co-heir with Christ!!!*"

It has been ingrained within church culture to look to Jesus as Savior, but rarely are they shown the Warrior Jesus. Not only does He come back in Revelation riding a horse with a sword coming out of His mouth, but even the Old Testament prophet Zephaniah reveals that The Warrior Jesus and The Savior are the same.

> *"The Lord your God is in your midst, A Warrior who saves. He will rejoice over you with joy; He will be quiet in His love [making no mention of your past sins], He will rejoice over you with shouts of joy." Zephaniah 3:17*

An intense war has been waged for your freedom and salvation. Although the outcome of this war has already been determined, **you must war in your mind and heart to come into line with the total victory.**

Jesus was The Great Warrior that defeated hell, death, and the grave to completely save you from your sin. He is furious in battle over your soul because you are that valuable. In the same way He is intense in warfare, He is passionate in the love and joy that He brings. God is not quiet in His love, but you are able to come into peace when He speaks The Word of Truth to your heart and soul.

When you come into line with His plans, purpose, and destiny, you will be walking in the same intense love, joy, and righteousness that He has won for you. This is how you will begin to walk as a Warrior of The Way. You must know The Way, walk in The Way, and ferociously love Jesus who is The Way, The Truth, and The Life (*John 14:6*). When you are in this place, you will not let any giant that comes against you stand in the way of walking in partnership with The Mighty Warrior, Commander of The Angel Armies!!!

Jesus, put on flesh and came to earth for you. His purpose was more than just to die for your sins. He lived a life of victory, died a death of victory, and rose again to victorious resurrected life. Every single day, you are called to live, die, and be reborn into victorious newness of life. You are to be armed with weapons of victory that have been given to you "*all power and authority in heaven and on earth*" (*Matt 28:18*).

When you walk and live in victory, any giant that will raise its head to come against you or your tribe will have to bow its knee. **You are no longer living for your own purpose and desire because there is no victory, power, or authority found in that place.** The victory is found in the overcoming of the enemy and taking new ground. When you are walking with the Victorious Warrior, He will lead you not only to slay every giant of this world, but He will lead you into your eternal inheritance and the divine destiny that God has for you.

Behind every giant is The Promised Land that is already yours if you will only go and take it. You will never be satisfied with the small portion where you are a slave when you have been given ownership of everything. You will overcome in every area while you are walking with The Commander of angel armies.

"Therefore, since Christ suffered in the flesh [and died for us], arm yourselves [like warriors] with the same purpose [being willing to suffer for doing what is right and pleasing God]..." 1 Peter 4:1

Jesus paid the price to overcome every speck of flesh that could ever raise itself against you. He suffered and died to Himself that you might live. In the same way, you must arm yourself like a warrior, and be willing to die to yourself, that you might overcome every obstacle and advance The Kingdom no matter what may stand in your way. **Every giant, stronghold, and obstacle must be removed so that you may walk into the fullness of the promise that has already been paid for by the very blood of Jesus.**

What is the point to slaying giants? A few reasons have already been discussed:

- *They inhabit The Promised Land*
- *They try to inhibit growth and movement in The Kingdom*
- *They stand directly opposed to the destiny plans and purposes that God has for you*
- *Because it is the nature of a Warrior of The Way*

Before this chapter is closed, I want to highlight another reason that giants must be slayed:

- *Giants prevent you from taking the mountains that God has given into your hands*

"Now therefore, give me this mountain of which the Lord spoke in that day; for you heard in that day how the Anakim were there, and that the cities were great and fortified. It may be that the Lord will be with me, and I shall be able to drive them out as the Lord

said." Joshua 14:12 (NKJV)

In the next chapter, more discussion in detail will take place about taking the mountains, but here are the words of Caleb. You have already read the words that he and Joshua brought back about the land being good and eating the giants for bread. This statement is spoken almost forty-five years later. Caleb is eighty-five and being asked to choose whatever part of the land that he desires. He has choice pick of the whole land, and what is his response? *"Give me the mountain of The Lord. Give me the fortified cities where giants live."*

How does this make sense? He should be retired and resting as one of the only two men left of the last generation. He and Joshua are the oldest of the entire population, and this is his request. God declares that Caleb has a different spirit within him than the rest of the people.

Caleb was not thinking it was time to rest and relax. He has been holding on to The Word of The Lord for more than forty years that God would give them this land. God would give them the mountains. He would give them the giants to eat like bread. He does not need to look with his physical eyes for the best looking land. **If God said this was what he was being given, it must be the best.** He had waited his entire lifetime to prove that God was able to do more than anyone could imagine, and this desire did not slacken with age. If anything, it became stronger and he became more adamant that God would prove himself to the next generation by allowing a senior to slay giants, take walled cities, and occupy the mountains. This might be impossible in the physical to accomplish, but God had said it was his inheritance if he would but possess it.

Caleb had complete and total faith that God would do what He said. They had been circling the mountain of The Lord in the wilderness, but **this was Caleb's mountain to conquer, occupy, and begin to build.**

In transitioning to the next chapter, I want to encourage you to spend some time with Holy Spirit asking for revelation of any giants that may be in your life and how to overcome them. Conquering these monsters is not just for your sake, but is vital to partner with the next generation to build and advance The Kingdom of God.

CHAPTER 7

TAKING MOUNTAINS

CROSSING OVER FROM the wilderness to The Promised Land, there will be giants that stand in your way. They were placed here to keep you from your destiny, and the purpose of The Lord: to possess the mountains.

> *"...The peaks of the mountains are His also."*
> **Psalm 95:4**

Every mountain was created as a place to encounter The Lord and rule with Him. At this moment, they may not be under the rulership of Jesus. The enemy understands the importance of these high places probably better than we do. The mountains are places of ruling, influence, encounter, and worship. If the enemy possesses these places illegally, he will be able to rule and influence from these positions of power. The mountains were never made for the enemy to rule over, but if they are not possessed by the people of God, the enemy will illegally occupy these strategic positions.

The Promised Land was possessed by an immoral, demonic people who served the plans and purposes of the enemy. They built strong walled cities and began to take uninhabited land while the inheritors were in bondage and wandering in the wilderness. It was never designed for the enemy and his forces. However, it was not taken and controlled by the sons of The Kingdom so it was ruled by the seed of the giants.

These unrighteous imposters influenced the people of the area until they came into bondage. Many, like Rahab, were just waiting to be freed from the tyranny and oppression but could never get freedom on their own. **For the strongholds to be torn down and the unrighteous kingdom to be dismantled, the sons of The Kingdom must slay the giants, occupy the mountains, and rule as righteous inheritors of The Promise.**

Anything unrighteous that occupies a mountain is an imposter. Every mountain must be brought into the Lordship of Christ!!!

THE MOUNTAIN MAN

> *"Then the [tribe of the] sons of Judah approached Joshua in Gilgal, and Caleb the son of Jephunneh the Kenizzite said to him, 'You know the word which the Lord said to Moses the man of God concerning me and you in Kadesh-barnea.'"*
> **Joshua 14:6**

Caleb says to Joshua, *"You know the word."* The Word of the Lord was not only spoken to them over forty years ago, they had been constantly reminding each other of this word. **They had heard, obeyed, held firmly, and declared this word over and over until it became a part of who they were.** When the time came to walk in it, both when they initially spied out the land and now much later, there was no hesitation to step fully into the promises that led to possessing the Promised Land of their inheritance. **No one and nothing would be able to stand in the way of them receiving all that God had spoken.**

Do you know the word that God has spoken over you?

Are you possessing the promises that will lead to your Promised Land?

Joshua and Caleb were sent into the land to spy it out and they brought back what was in their heart. Ten spies came back with fear, intimidation, and doubt, but these two came back more full of faith than ever before. **What they saw with their natural eyes were enemy giants illegally occupying their promised inheritance.** They brought back what was in their heart and were rewarded with carrying and possessing the promise until the hearts and minds of the people were changed. When this transformation finally took place, they were ready to lead people into the promises no matter what opposition might stand against them.

Moses declared their inheritance at the time Joshua and Caleb took their stand of faith. Everywhere their feet had touched would be theirs. Even though this was promised before the whole people, Joshua and Caleb had to carry this within them for forty years in the wilderness. **They had to constantly place themselves in the presence of The Promise Giver and declare what He had spoken over them.** This life of faith outlasted every doubting man that had spoken what they could see instead of what God had said.

In the end, the carnal, fleshly generation that walked according to the wisdom of the world and that judged by what their eyes could see, passed away. The Word of The Lord remained. **As Joshua and Caleb fastened their faith to The Word, they were carried into longevity, strength, wisdom, leadership, greatness, and legacy.** They are the only ones remembered of the generation that succeeded Moses. No one else is even named. **Joshua and Caleb became the fathers and leaders of the generation because they continued to speak and walk in the Word of The Lord** no matter what they saw, heard, or felt that might make them believe the contrary.

In the wilderness, Moses went in and out of The Presence of The Lord to get The Word and speak it to the people. The people would not go in and receive it themselves because of fear and doubt. This entire generation was not allowed to cross over into the promised land. However, Joshua stayed in the presence of the Lord (*Exodus 33:11*).

Because of the position Caleb takes later, I believe he was there as well. He was the unknown, barely named one. You do not see him leading the military or sitting at the right hand of Moses. You do not see him being trained up to lead people. However, you see that before and after he went into the land, over the course of forty years, **his heart and spirit remain in line with the promise.** There is only one way that this could take place in the middle of a doubt-filled, rebellious people, **he was constantly placing himself in The Presence.**

History-makers, world-shakers, and generational leaders do not come out of the masses in a moment. They are trained, equipped, and set apart for years in the unknown before they are given the ability to step into their promise. These must remain with the Promise Giver and the Destiny Designer. **The closer you are with Him, the more He will trust you to carry out The Word that He has spoken over you.** As you walk out the promises spoken to you, you will be entrusted to carry other promises given to many people, and even generations, that never stepped into the fullness.

Caleb was the son of Jephunneh which means "He will turn to or face." I believe that Caleb's grandfather truly turned to face The Lord fully. He named his son after this decision to face The Lord and pursue the promise. This legacy was passed down to Caleb who is known for nothing else, but his willingness to possess The Promised Land no matter what.

The name Caleb is believed to be a shortened form of, "*Chelubai,*" which means "the binding together of The Lord, interwoven with The Lord." Just as Jephunneh's destiny was called out by his name, so Caleb's purpose was claimed in his name. **He was continually being called out to be bound together and interwoven with The Lord.** This is what his father instilled within him.

As Caleb grew and eventually was chosen to be the one to search out The Promised Land, God said he had a different spirit within him. **He came back and spoke The Word of The Lord because he had The Spirit of The Living God interwoven throughout his life, and it could**

not be separated. The unclean spirit of fear could not overpower the interwoven Spirit of God that became who Caleb was. Therefore, at the age of forty-five or eighty-five, the spirit was the same Spirit, eternal, undying, unchanging, everlasting.

This is the same Spirit that lives and indwells you if you are living as a son. You **too are to become interwoven with The Spirit.** This is the only way to enter into the fullness of your eternal destiny, plan, and promised land. It begins with the turning of your face to The Lord.

No matter where you may be, whether in bondage or in the wilderness, as you turn to face The Lord more and more and place yourself in His presence, you will become increasingly interwoven with His Spirit. This will enable you to advance into the Promised Land that has already been given to you.

> (Caleb says) *"Now, here I am this day, eighty-five years old. As yet I am as strong this day as on the day that Moses sent me; just as my strength was then, so now is my strength for war, both for going out and for coming in."*
> *Joshua 14:11* (NKJV)

The strength of the promise did not diminish because of time. **The promises of God are timeless and ever ready for the taking. The moment you begin to step into the promise, you will be given everything you need to walk it out.** Caleb kept this promise alive in his spirit until it came time to be tested again. Once again, he stood firm on The Word he had been given. He never wavered or doubted even though he was well past fighting age. God had kept him healthy, whole, and strong that he might walk into the fullness of the promise.

> *"Now therefore, give me this mountain of which the Lord spoke in that day; for you heard in that day how the Anakim were there, and that the cities were great and fortified."*
> *Joshua 14:12* (NKJV)

This is an important point to note. The Lord spoke of the mountain. This was not some whimsical thing that they came up with that it would be fun to possess a mountain. Joshua and Caleb went in and spied out the land. While there, they were listening for what God would say and watching for what He would do. All the other spies looked with their physical eyes and began to agree with the wisdom of the world. Caleb and Joshua looked for what God was saying about the giants and their fortified cities.

It does not take a son to state the obvious and see the problem; however, **a son will look to see what The Father is saying about the situation.** You need to begin to see past the wilderness, giants, troubles, and trials. If you stop at seeing the negative, you have not even begun to live as a son. You must look to Father God for the wisdom of heaven and what His perspective is on the situation.

Looking eye to eye, the people were like grasshoppers compared to the monstrous mammoths in the land. Looking from heaven, they were bread to be chewed up and consumed. They found out from Rahab that the people of the land had already been defeated in their minds and hearts by simply hearing of the power of God's mighty works. All the people of God had to do was walk in and finish what He had already begun doing since they walked out of Egypt.

Sadly, the enemy's tactic of fear and intimidation worked and delayed the promise of God. Caleb and Joshua were the only ones to stand and intercede for their generation. When all the people came to silence them, God spoke from heaven and put an end to their nonsense.

The entire generation of unbelievers could not walk into a promised land because of fear. But a new generation was arising! This generation was captained by two men of faith. They were untried and untested. However, **the wilderness of judgment for the doubting generation, became the training ground for the next.** The people of God would have their own decision to make when they were called to march into the Promised Land.

Caleb and Joshua's inheritance was delayed, but it was not diminished or destroyed. In fact, **they had the opportunity to multiply the inheritance by training the next generation to step into their fullness.** These two had the faith to go in and gain their inheritance the first time they entered the land. However, they knew that the land was promised to a generation, and it was only through partnering with all the people that the fullness of the inheritance could be possessed for ages to come. Their patient waiting, sowing, and willingness to return to the wilderness made Joshua and Caleb true fathers to the next generation. Because of faithfulness to The Promise, Joshua and Caleb not only received their abundant reward, but generations were blessed by their faith and steadfastness.

> *"Hebron therefore became the inheritance of Caleb the son of Jephunneh the Kenizzite to this day, because he wholly followed the Lord God of Israel. And the name of Hebron formerly was Kirjath Arba (Arba was the greatest man among the Anakim). Then the land had rest from war."*
> **Joshua 14:14-15** (NKJV)

When Caleb goes up to take *Kirjath-Arba*, it is stated that *Arba* is the father or greatest of the giants. He is probably not still around, but Caleb defeats three of his sons. Caleb, this "nobody" with no real family legacy, partnered with the promise of The Lord and took the greatest giant stronghold that was home to the greatest warrior and his children. Caleb did much more than just talk a good talk. He chose the biggest and best of the giants and the greatest fortified city to take in accordance with The Word of The Lord. He easily overcomes whatever resistance was there, so much so there is no record of a battle. He forces the giants out or kills them and this becomes his headquarters.

God is pleased with Caleb's faithfulness to the promise, and Hebron becomes one of the most famous cities. Throughout the Bible it is named as:

- A place that Abraham formerly built an altar to the Lord (*Gen 13:18*)

- A place that God visited Abraham to reveal the promise of Isaac (*Gen 18:1*)

- The place where Sarah died and was perhaps buried (*Gen 23:2*)

- The place where Isaac was buried (*Gen 35:27*)

- The place where Jacob was buried (*Gen 47:30*)

- This was literally the place Caleb spied out originally (*Num 13:22*)

- A holy city of the Levites (*Josh 21:11*)
- A city of refuge (*Josh 21:13*)
- David was anointed as king here and ruled for seven years (*2 Sam 2:4*)

When Abraham, the carrier of The Promise, came into the land, he built an altar. Hebron was the place where this altar was built. The blessing was given here. Not only that, past faithful generations that walked in and carried the promise rested here in the ground.

Hebron was a place of great blessing. When the people of God left, the enemy came in quickly and built his stronghold here. Whether he was trying to steal the blessing for himself or block the people of God from accessing this blessing, he knew this was a blessed place. Caleb did not necessarily know the fullness of this blessing, however, he had a word from The Lord. **This was his inheritance and he would settle for nothing less.** Because of this, Hebron, when taken by Caleb, was dedicated to the Lord as a holy place for the Levites, a city of righteousness and refuge, and a city of kings. Because Caleb tapped into The Promise, he received the fullness of the blessing that rested in this place. **Generations were blessed because of his faithfulness.**

The very next action that takes place proves how much Caleb has heard The Word of The Lord. After he captures the walled city of giants, Caleb gives the next generation the opportunity to step into the same promise.

"Caleb said, 'I will give Achsah my daughter as wife to the man who attacks Kiriath-sepher and captures it.'"
Joshua 15:16

Caleb offers a great reward to whomever would partner with the promise to destroy the giants and take the fortified cities. His nephew Othniel answers the call quickly and easily overcomes. It does not say specifically, but it is quite probable that Othniel was like his son. Caleb's brother would have died in the wilderness with the generation that did not believe. Both Caleb's nephew and daughter understand inheritance in a way that could only be imparted by a man of faith.

Othniel (meaning, "Lion, God is a force, or word of God") not only receives the daughter and the city, but begins to walk in the blessing that Caleb has tapped into. After the elder leaders had passed away and the people of God are in trouble, because they forsook the promise, Othniel was infused with The Spirit of The Lord. He delivers the land from oppression and gives them 40 years of peace (*Judges 3:9-11*). He is actually redeeming the curse of 40 years wandering in the wilderness in disobedience. **He is able to tap into a generational blessing and become a judge, leader, and blessing for the entire nation.** He brings the blessing to a generation whereas Caleb released the blessing upon a city and his descendants.

THE MOUNTAINS

Throughout the scriptures, the importance of mountains can easily be seen, and the ones that ruled them. When the people of God walked in righteousness, the mountains were fruitful, abundant and blessings upon all the people. They were places of worship, joy, proclamation and the very presence of God. If these places were uninhabited or ruled by unrighteous peoples, pain, destruction, and death were multiplied throughout the land.

In *Genesis 36:8-9*, Esau dwelt in the mountains of Seir. As one who walked in his own selfish desires and lusts of the flesh, these mountains became known for these things.

What rules you will rule the mountain that you take!!!

Seir literally means "gate of horror and violence." This was what was in Esau's heart when he began to rule. He wanted to inflict violence upon his brother because of his own fleshly failings and lustful desires. He had given away a kingly inheritance for a bowl of beans. Now, he would take it back by force. The seed of the enemy was already within his heart. Undealt with, this became what ruled the mountain that Esau inhabited. The enemy desires to take mountains for his control. Esau is known as Edom, and this becomes Mount Edom.

Just as Edom means "red, blood, and to produce," this mountain known as the gate of horror and violence becomes the mountain that produces red blood. Generations would look to this place ruled by wickedness, and they would fear what came from here.

However, in *Numbers 24:18* generations later, a prophetic word is given that The Messiah will take control of Seir. The remnant of violence that gained power and ruled this mountain for so long will be completely destroyed and placed under Messiah's feet. The people will take this mountain and claim it for The Kingdom by the power of righteous blood.

In *Obadiah*, the mountains of Edom are being judged because of their violence and unrighteousness. Pride has caused its false masters to make their home in the secure heights and set themselves up as lofty rulers. The wisdom, might, treasure, worldly alliance and power they gained through violence and murder will be cut off because of pride and arrogance and resistance to The Lord.

Their complacency (doing nothing), compliance (agreeing and rejoicing in), and collaboration (actively helping) with the destruction of the people of God is their sin. Violence and murder has ruled this mountain long enough as judgment is pronounced by the prophet.

God's people who rule from Zion will turn Edom from the destroy-

ers into the deliverers. Every enemy will be slaughtered as they have slaughtered others. The people of God will deliver the land from this violence and false rulership.

When this mountain is brought into The Kingdom by the people of God, they gain not only the mountain, but the plains, fields, land across the river, and many cities . **This mountain was the key to all these places.** When taken for The Kingdom and brought into righteous judgment, advancement for The Kingdom and The Kingship of The Lord was given over the entire area. **This mountain was the key to ruling the entire region!!!**

In *1 Kings 18*, the prophet Elijah comes out of the wilderness. Not much is known about him, his background, or lineage. All that is known is that **he is moving at The Word of The Lord.**

You too must learn to live and move according to The Word of The Lord! Your background, past reputation, or family reputation do not propel you forward. Only The Word and Promise of The Lord will carry you into your eternal destiny and calling.

Elijah comes on the scene when the land is in great turmoil. Ahab and Jezebel have turned over everything to their false demon gods and have submitted the entire nation to this bondage. Mount Carmel means "fruitful field," but there is no fruitfulness in the land when it is ruled by the enemy. In fact, there were several years of famine as a result of the submission of this place to demons. The Word of the Lord is that this mountain is designed to be fruitful. It can only enter into its eternal destiny when taken for The Kingdom.

All the people were so confused and leaderless that they said not a word when the prophet spoke The Word of the Lord. They did not understand or know who was truly God. They had completely lost their way. **The prophet had to come, speak, declare, and obey for the fruitful field of The Kingdom to break open once again.**

Elijah heard The Word. He spoke it. He believed it. He obeyed it. This was what made him different. He may have been seemingly standing alone, but he was standing with the Word. **You must learn to stand with The Word, and line yourself up with Him completely, no matter the opposition.**

There is no fruit in the valley of indecision. **The fruitful field is on the mountain when ruled by the one who stands on The Lord's side and is willing to stand in the fire!!!** Elijah went to the mountain to reclaim ownership of the fruitful field. When Baal ruled the mountain there was drought, but one son, standing in The Promise, returned the rightful reign. When God ruled the fruitful field, rain came in abundance as a result!!!

Where does The Word need to reign in your life?

Elijah came and proved beyond all doubt that God ruled this mountain. Elijah executed every demonic entity that could ever seek to rise again. Anything left undealt with would rise again to seduce and pervert a fat, lazy, and weak-minded people. **Only those burning with the Fire had the ability to rule the mountain in righteousness.**

Partnering with the promise, Elijah easily overcame every enemy. Following this, he got burned out and afraid because he had no one to pass the baton to. **Just as you cannot take the mountain on your own, you cannot maintain it by yourself.** The sons must come together and rule the territory that has been taken from the enemy. You were never meant to walk on your own. Elijah quickly became tired and discouraged because he felt like he was the only one standing.

Because of this, he was open to intimidation by the principality that ruled. Jezebel spoke and attacked the prophet. In his weakness, he began to seek the fresh word to strengthen him. The Word of The Lord is designed not to keep for yourself, but to multiply in fruit and scope. Elijah took the mountain, but to set the region free a partnership and unity had to take place. **The legacy of The Kingdom is to take the mountain and rule for generations.**

When the Word of The Lord is spoken Elijah recognizes his weakness and begins to build according to The Word of The Lord that he received on the mountain. He is immediately directed to anoint three individuals (*1 Kings 19:15-17*): Hazael, Jehu and Elisha. Somewhere in the process of anointing these and passing the baton to Elisha, Elijah also raised up an army of prophets.

Within the names of these people God calls Elijah to anoint, there is a clear message. The first is Hazael, the king (of Syria) which means, *"seer or one who sees God."* **The first step is to begin to see the word, picture, or promise that God is speaking.** This is the prophetic vision and destiny of what is designed to take place.

Next, Elijah is to anoint Jehu, the warrior, which means, *"He is God."* **Once the vision or promise is seen, The Truth must be spoken out.** It is not enough to only see and know, but a prophetic declaration must take place that The Promise may be established.

Finally, Elijah is called to anoint Elisha, the prophet, whose name means, *"God is my Salvation."* **After the promise or vision is seen and declared, it must be carried out in obedience.** This may take an extended period of time and work depending on the size of The Word.

The God-sized vision is not something you can accomplish on your own, but must be infused into the next generation to carry and multiply. God does not design anything to be temporary. **God's purpose is eternal increase and never-ending advancement.** This can only take place as each new generation is inspired and infused with The Word. As this foundation is built upon, fresh promises and insight will propel them to expansion and multiplication that could take place no other way.

Put simply, you must:

- *See the Word.*
- *Say The Word.*
- *Do The Word.*
- *Teach the Word.*

Within the prophetic vision in *Jeremiah 4*, the prophet is calling for a banner to be raised toward Mount Zion. Mount Zion is where the presence of The Lord rules, reigns, and rests in righteousness. Safety, victory, and life are under The Lord who reigns here. This is the end result of bringing the mountains into the dominion of the Kingdom. The presence of The Lord rules from Mount Zion. **Your King calls you to rule the mountains where you are and place them under His dominion.**

A proclamation of evil comes from Mount Ephraim. The fruitfulness that this mountain was appointed to bring to the people has been perverted into a multiplication of evil and judgment. Righteousness did not rule the fruitful mountain. Because of this, righteous rewards of safety, victory, and life are not multiplied, but rather judgment, tragedy, and doom.

This is not the plan or purpose of The Lord. He has purposed for fruitful abundance of righteous reward to come forth. However, **when the mountain, region, area where you reside is not taken for The Kingdom, it will be perverted for evil purposes.** The enemy knows the power of ruling the mountains and will begin to bring in giants and build generational strongholds for as long as the people of God draw back in fear or complacency. *"We are not of those who draw back in fear, but those who believe to the full salvation, deliverance, and healing of the body, mind, and soul"* (**Heb 10:39**). The result of living in this place of freedom in The Presence is regions being set free into their God-ordained destiny and the eternal advancement of The Kingdom!!!

In *Jeremiah 4*, you see that the mountains were trembling at the anger of the Lord. **The presence of The Lord directly affects the mountains.** Just as evil and unrighteousness will pervert the influence of these mountains, so the presence of The Kingdom brings them back into order. The wilderness was changed into fertile land when the fierce anger of The Lord destroyed the wickedness.

No matter what your region, or mountain looks like presently, the dynamic potential of The Presence is to transform darkness into light by the ones whose hearts are burning with the fire of The Lord. The light within you will dispel every dark thing if you do not lose heart or turn tail and run. Having done all to stand, stand firm! Help is on the way! You are not alone!

God's vision and purposes have been crying out from the ground for the sons of God to take dominion and rule as regents within The Kingdom. **All those who are placing themselves in the service of The King are being trained to overtake, overthrow, and overwhelm the enemy on every side.** Help is on the way!!!

In *Matthew 17*, Jesus leads his inner circle, Peter, James and John, up on a high mountain. Here, He is transfigured, communes with saints in the heavenly cloud, and hears the voice of God. This is a discipleship moment. **As Jesus possesses the mountain, new realms are opened for Him and those with Him.**

The three have their eyes and ears opened in a new way. **New encouragement and new revelation come on the mountain.** What is revealed in this place, is not for Jesus or the Three's personal benefit alone. They are to take what they have received, grow, and go.

Vision, revelation and encouragement are not enough to walk out the gospel. They are immediately presented with an opportunity to apply what they have received. Jesus puts the revelation into practice completely and easily conquers the enemy. The disciples are still living in old ways, mindsets, and revelation. **Lack of faith in The Word spoken leads to powerless people.**

Faith that destroys doubt, mixed with revelation and encouragement, will cause mountains to be moved. God spoke exactly what was needed for that moment. If they had received, believed and walked in this revelation they would have been able to do what Jesus did.
Prayer and fasting is a key, a lost relic, to dominate flesh and remove the doubt and opinions of your heart and of others that influence you. You must position yourself in the best possible way to receive the spiritual words of life from Heaven and walk them out. If you do not, you will never be able to possess the mountains or receive the new levels of revelation and power that come from ruling them.

> *"Now the eleven disciples went to Galilee, to the mountain which Jesus had designated... Jesus came up and said to them, 'All authority (all power of absolute rule) in heaven and on earth has been given to Me.'"*
> **Matthew 28:16,18**

It is on this specific mountain that Jesus releases not only the good news of His resurrection, but also transmits the fullness of The Kingdom. **Jesus declares all authority has been given to Him and is your inheritance as His disciple.** Even as He empowered the disciples, He released and commanded them to go into all the nations making disciples everywhere.

> *"Go therefore and make disciples of all the nations, baptizing them in the name of the Father and of the Son and of the Holy Spirit, teaching them to observe all things that I have commanded you; and lo, I am with you always, even to the end of the age."*
> **Matthew 28:19-20** (NKJV)

The ever-abiding presence of Jesus is declared and promised on the mountain. Then, Jesus is taken into Heaven. This might cause one to question what Jesus has just spoken (... *lo, I am with you always even to the end of the age"*).

If Jesus is always with them, why does He leave?

Jesus is instituting a spiritual principle of the heavenly mountain of Zion on a physical mountain. He releases a revelation of a spiritual mountain and the ruling and reigning of His sons from this place. Not the physical mountain, but the mountain of Zion.

Mount Zion is fully established by Jesus on the earth. In this realm, the sons receive power and authority to advance and overthrow demonic principalities, strongholds, and illegitimately inhabited mountains. The spiritual rules over the physical. However, there is a link to physical and spiritual mountains that is perpetuated by the ascension, and eventual return, of Jesus at this place.

What is the point?

You must go up Mount Zion, where the presence of The Lord is. You will rule and reign spiritually from this place, and you receive everything you need from the voice of God. After this, the power comes upon you to carry this presence into the deepest, darkest parts of this world and overthrow the illegitimate rulers.

The ever-increasing Kingdom of God comes as His sons realize who they are and assume the position of ruling and reigning. They carry this mountain of authority and power wherever they need to overthrow an unauthorized spiritual ruler. In order to increase The Kingdom, you must constantly be training others to step into their spiritual designation as sons and reign in the authority that they have been given.

In *Hebrews 12:18-29,* Mount Zion is the spiritual place where God and His people dwell. This is the place that The Word is spoken, revealed, and sent. **This Word shakes both Heaven and earth because they are spoken from a place of power and authority. These revealed words are what change and transform you.** As you are transformed into a son, you too are given this right to rule and reign with The Word spoken from the place of authority and power.

As The Word is spoken, a shaking takes place. This Word is the original design of The Creator and is directly opposed to the fleshly structures that have been built by the rulers of this world. **Shaken things will be changed by the fire of The Lord.** The fire is the word, power, and love of The Lord. This is what will cause change to occur when it goes forth from Zion.

The only things that are able to remain are those that have gone through the forge (consuming fire of The Lord). **Refining, reshaping, and reordering are necessary for The Kingdom of The Lord to be built.** All this takes place when the sons ascend into The Presence in Mount Zion and are transformed themselves in The Presence by The Word. They must continually speak this Word faithfully and truthfully from their place of power and authority and watch as the kingdoms of this world are shaken and transformed into The Kingdom of God.

Mount Zion is the key to taking every other mountain in the earth. Worldly structures melt in The Presence. *Hebrews 12* speaks about discipline, righteousness, and the love of The Father for His sons. **You must go through the forge that will burn away the fleshly things of this world in order to be transformed into a son that rules in the power and authority of The Word.** This can only happen as you constantly place yourself in The Presence and allow yourself to be shaped, molded, and ordered by The Lord. **The forge is for you first that you may become a true representative of The Kingdom.** Then, you can be used to declare The Word and dispatch the fire of The Lord for the taking and transforming of mountains, cities, regions, and peoples.

In *Revelation 14:1-5*, The Lamb of God, the Perfect Sacrifice, The Resurrection and The Life is established on Mount Zion with 144,000 chosen people. **The Conqueror rules Mount Zion with the sons.** These are the chosen, ransomed, redeemed people of God. These are His followers, the first fruits of the people of God. They are marked, set apart, and holy people.

Steadfast endurance is the defining characteristic of God's people. They habitually keep God's commandments and their faith in Him. Perseverance and long suffering to the end. Nothing can stop them, nothing can hold them back. What you do in this life will continue into eternity. **You were designed to rule and reign from Zion with The King in the heavenly realm and bring this reality to earth.**

You will be marked either by God or Babylon. There is no middle ground! Babylon is the way of this world and the system and structure of this world. Ruling by wealth, power, manipulation and control is the corrupt way of this world. **The people of God will rule from Mount Zion and bring His Kingdom to earth.** Every mountain that stands before The King will be brought low and bow before Zion and The King of Kings, El Shaddai, God of The Mountain!!!

The concept of Mount Zion is continually built upon by the prophets and those that can see into the heavenly, ruling realm. Everything on the earth is affected as the sons take their place in this spiritual mountain. **Every other mountain will be overcome by those who know their power and authority comes from being in the Presence on The Mountain.** His Kingdom will fill the whole earth. You must partner with Him from this place to bring about a radical transformation. This is the *"on earth as it is in heaven"* reality that the sons long to see made manifest right here, and right now.

> *"The wilderness and the dry land will be glad; The Arabah (desert) will shout in exultation and blossom Like the autumn crocus. It will blossom abundantly And rejoice with joy and singing. The glory of Lebanon will be given to it, The majesty of [Mount] Carmel and [the plain] of Sharon. They will see the glory of the Lord, The majesty and splendor of our God."*
> **Isaiah 35:1-2**

Even though you may be walking through a wilderness and dry land, this is not where you were designed to stay. Not only are you created to walk through the wilderness, but you are to come to realize your original design and gain the identity of a son as you journey through this place. As you place yourself in The Presence on The Mountain, you will begin to rule and reign in the inheritance that you have been given. As you do this, what was once the wilderness and desert will begin to bear fruit. You will see that even in the dark times, when you were going through the fires of the forge, God was training and using you to plant the seed that would bear fruit even in this seemingly hard and dark place.

The joy of The Lord will come to these places that were once fields of death and dying. **As you look back over the rugged path you have traversed, you will be able to see the resurrection life that has been infused within your soul.** Not only was this strengthening happening inside of you, but also those around you, that looked at these trying times and saw the glory of God raising you up from the ashes. They will be able to see and declare the goodness and glory of God. **The Lord never wastes anything.** Increase is your portion even in the times when all you see is darkness and death. **Multiplication and increase are the son's portion if you will continue to press into The Presence of The Lord.**

> *"Encourage the exhausted, and make staggering knees firm.*
> *Say to those with an anxious and panic-stricken heart, 'Be strong,*
> *fear not! Indeed, your God will come with vengeance [for the*
> *ungodly]; The retribution of God will come, But He will save you.'"*
> **Isaiah 35:3-4**

As you come to the place of gladness and begin to walk in the power and authority you have been given as a ruling son, it is important that you continue to reproduce. Many are trapped in the wilderness and have fallen to the wayside. Some have become wounded in the battle and are struggling to continue on. Religious demons have lured some off track, and they have become weak trying to walk in the way or take mountains in their own strength. Some do not have a clear understanding of the inheritance of a son and have exhausted themselves trying to earn the Promised Land that they have already been given.

As a son, you must continually encourage, strengthen, and disciple the people of God needing help that are revealed to you. **You must not become complacent, but return continuously to the wilderness to bring aid, hope, and life to everyone who needs it.** The giant of pride would love to come in and pervert the heart of a son and make him think that he is better than any other person who is struggling through the wilderness. As a son, you must always remember that every single son is *"raised up to be seated in heavenly places"* (**Eph 2:6**).

Not one person deserves to be a son. You must come into your inheritance by the blood of Jesus, the perfect sacrifice. You are not better because you may be farther along in maturity or in a different place. **Everything is a gift and grace that you have been given. This same gift is available to any that would seek it.** The joy of others coming out of darkness, into light, and walking in fulfillment of their call will cause you to reproduce what you have been given continually in others, especially those who need it most.

> *"Then the eyes of the blind will be opened And the ears of the deaf will be unstopped. Then the lame will leap like a deer, And the tongue of the mute will shout for joy. For waters will break forth in the wilderness And streams in the desert."*
> **Isaiah 35:5-6**

As a son, you are called to place yourself in the middle of the deepest darkest circumstances. **The light within you will dispel darkness only when it is brought into the dark places.** You are not a light to continuously remain in a place where light is all around. You will shine the brightest in the darkest and most hidden places. Blind eyes cannot be opened if there are no spiritually or physically blind people around you. You must go to where they are and step out in faith that the Kingdom may be advanced in the supposedly hardest and darkest places. Only those who are looking with their physical eyes and walking in worldly wisdom will see the hard and dark. **The sons see more area to be taken for The Kingdom. They see another mountain to be conquered, another giant to be consumed, and more hungry people waiting for The Truth of the gospel to show up.** There are more eyes and ears that have been saturated in darkness waiting for the light of the gospel to shine bright and bring revelation to those who have been in bondage. Those who have been unable to move because of imprisonment and oppression will leap with joy at the proclamation of the gospel. Closed mouths will be opened wide with joyful exaltation and evangelistic speech when the power of God brings the transformation they were so desperate for without even knowing.

The wilderness and deserts of this world have trapped people for far too long. Weights, troubles, cares, depression, fear… have been the giants that have enslaved the people who have not yet seen the light. **When the sons release the vision from Zion, speak the words of life, and actively carry this back into the deserts and wilderness; waters, streams, and fruitful fields cannot help but abound.** All the lost, hurting, and enslaved will rejoice when the sons of The King declare his Kingdom advancing in every area. **The darkness is dispelled when the sons of light come on the scene.** It is time to rule and reign from the Mountain in the very Presence and carry what you have received into a world waiting for transformation and translation into The Kingdom.

> *"And the burning sand (mirage) will become a pool [of water] And the thirsty ground springs of water; In the haunt of jackals, where they lay resting, Grass becomes reeds and rushes. A highway will be there, and a roadway; And it will be called the Holy Way. The unclean will not travel on it, But it will be for those who walk on the way [the redeemed]; And fools will not wander on it."*
> **Isaiah 35:7-8**

Out of nothing and the imaginations of the heart will spring forth true life giving substance. No matter the dreams or visions that you had before, none could compare to what God will make manifest even in the middle of the wilderness, desert, and land of famine. **Fruitfulness always comes when you go up Mount Zion.** Not a thing is wasted. No effort, sacrifice, dream or vision will perish when the sons of God are seated in Zion. Dry and thirsty hearts will bring forth fruit and life in a way that will come no other way but ruling from the mountain. Even the beasts and giants of the land cannot stop the ruling sons from Zion. Though they try to cause death and decay, this is just fertilizer for what God is causing to spring forth. Their decapitated bodies will become the fuel for the fruitful field of the former wilderness.

What was once uninhabited wasteland, a valley of the shadow of death will be built into a highway of holiness. **The Wilderness Way is built by sons ruling from Zion and taking the Promised Land from the enemy.** Pioneers, forerunners, and wilderness explorers are those who see the fruit in the desert. These know that no matter how the enemy has destroyed and robbed from the land that he had illegitimately governed, fruit and harvest are just waiting for the righteous, redeemed sons to call forth the seeds to rise up from the ground. A slain enemy becomes the fertilizer for the fruitful field of the Lord. The bodies of the enemy become a pathway for others to enter into The Presence, and find their way to Zion.

Those whose eyes are darkened by the enemy cannot find the way in the wilderness. Only those who have been transferred into the Kingdom and whose eyes have been opened to the One who reigns in Zion will find this pathway. This is the road that continually leads to Zion from wherever the people of God set their focus to claim The Kingdom. There is always a way made to return to the presence and reign from Zion.

Those who are healed and whole in His presence will go out into the darkest places and take the more forbidden mountains as a precious gift for the King in Zion. **The harder the mountain, the greater the harvest is, and the more valuable the gift becomes.** The King is worthy of every mountain, valley, wilderness and desert. These are all His Kingdom and are waiting for the sons to activate the seeds of The Kingdom that have lain dormant for generations. **The presence of the sons unlocks the fruitfulness of the land!!!**

> *"No lion will be there, Nor will any predatory animal come up on it; They will not be found there. But the redeemed will walk there. And the ransomed of the Lord will return And come to Zion with shouts of jubilation, And everlasting joy will be upon their heads; They will find joy and gladness, And sorrow and sighing will flee away."*
> *Isaiah 35:9-10*

No destroying enemy is able to walk in The Way. No giant, or wild ravenous beast can be in this place. The untamed animals cannot stand against the Lion of Judah and His sons. **Those that have walked in The Presence of The Lion of Judah will destroy every enemy that comes close to this path.** There will be no foxes to spoil this vine, no scavengers to consume, no weak or sickly stragglers. **The sons hunt the deadly lions.** The hungry consume the enemy. Giants become their bread, and the wilderness becomes a fruitful field. **Overtaken strongholds of the enemy become the refuge and fortresses of The King.** The righteous and redeemed remnant will rule and reign.

The darkness of surrounding circumstances, the depression of the past, or obstacles of the enemy will never hinder the hungry sons from returning to Mount Zion and receiving the Living Word to implant the seeds of the promise into the Promised Land. **This hidden harvest and subterranean treasure will spring forth and multiply the work of The Kingdom.** Joy, jubilation, and the pleasures of the Promised Land are multiplied abundantly as this harvest begins to bring more sons to Mount Zion to reign. Sons are revealed, and The Kingdom will advance as mountains are placed at the feet of Jesus as crowns and gifts. **The harvest of generations is waiting for sons to lay claim to their rightful territory and advance to take it from the giants and beasts that have illegally laid claim to it.** All the mountains, valleys, fields, and subterranean treasures are the rightful inheritance of the King and the sons of Mount Zion!

All the mountains are the Lord's, and all the treasures underneath. For far too long, the enemy has illegally occupied mountains, valleys, and hidden treasuries because a weak and ineffective people have seen them and been scared. **No longer! The mighty sons are arising!** The mountain strongholds and subterranean treasuries are not only their inheritance, but their desire to capture, overthrow, and lay before The King as an offering.

The people struggling in bondage because of cruel taskmasters will be freed, led into the Kingdom, and raised up to rule and reign in the very places that they were in bondage so long ago. The inheritance is for all those who would come to The King and hunger for the freedom and legacy that He is eagerly waiting to present to His children.

> *"Ask and keep on asking and it will be given to you; seek and keep on seeking and you will find; knock and keep on knocking and the door will be opened to you. For everyone who keeps on asking receives, and he who keeps on seeking finds, and to him who keeps*

on knocking, it will be opened... If you then, evil (sinful by nature) as you are, know how to give good and advantageous gifts to your children, how much more will your Father who is in heaven [perfect as He is] give what is good and advantageous to those who keep on asking Him."
Matthew 7:7-8,11

Now is the time to ask!

Now the time to seek!

Now is the time to knock!

Now is the time to advance!!!

CHAPTER 8
ADVANCING THE KINGDOM

MOSES AND THE people had been delivered from slavery by the signs, wonders, and miracles that were done by The Lord. Just as He had promised, He led them out of Egypt and was taking them through the wilderness to the Promised Land. Every last person left Egypt knowing that they would live and die for generations in slavery if they stayed. However, as soon as hardship and trouble came, they were eager to turn back to this life of bondage and destruction.

Whether you have been on the journey on The Wilderness Way or have begun to possess some part of your inheritance in The Promised Land, **there will always be the temptation to settle where you are or return to the easy way. Inheriting the promise is not easy.** Every part of your flesh wants to be satiated with the easy carnal things. However you will never get to the Promised Land, slay giants, take mountains, or walk in the generational legacy that God has for you following your own way.

> *"And the Lord said to Moses, 'Why do you cry to Me? Tell the children of Israel to go forward.'"*
> ***Exodus 14:15***

The Word of The Lord is "*Advance!!!*", "*Go Forward!!!*" At this moment, The Word and the presence of The Lord had led them to camp in front of the sea. They are in front of one of the major demonic rulers of the region, baal-zephon. They were in enemy territory, escaped slaves, with the sea in front of them, and an army of chariots behind them. *What was their response?*

They began to complain. The people are crying out against God and accusing Him of leading them to their death. Moses is crying out to God for their salvation and rescue. There is literally no escape. They are hemmed in on all sides. The Word of the Lord comes. "*Advance*". "*Go forward into the sea!*"

When God speaks, often, it will not make sense to you. Moses seems to be the only one speaking and acting out the Word of faith. **One man siding with the Lord is the majority.** He is told to lift his staff and stretch out his hand, simple, easy obedience. But put yourself in Moses' position. The ruling power of the world at the time, who is now your bitter enemy, is behind. I would have wanted to stretch my staff toward the enemy to part the enemy. Maybe toward the demonic idol to split the idol in two. But that was not the way forward. One path led forward to The Mountain of The Lord and His inheritance. **Through the seemingly impassable obstacle was the way forward.**

At that moment, Moses had to decide again to believe and obey The Word of The Lord.

What about you?

What has God spoken to you that does not make sense?

What prophetic word have you been given that you have not acted on?

Too many times you can look at these as detached stories from history and not apply them to your own life. The people of God, the inheritors of The Promise, you and I are called to advance The Kingdom of God in every area.

In the middle of writing this book, our family was given a word, first spoken to my six-year old, it is time to move. Although we had been praying about this move for about three years, it made no sense in the natural. My wife and I were near our families and the hometowns where we grew up and knew everyone. Although I had traveled extensively for missions, I had never really lived anywhere else. I was making the most money I ever had and the connections in ministry were there in the great state of Texas. *Why would we ever want to go anywhere else?*

When The Word came, it was *"Go, and go quickly!"* We were told to advance, pack up, and move in six weeks. Knowing this was a word from The Lord, we set our hearts to obey. Six weeks later, we began the journey. Everything we had was packed into a small trailer behind my truck. I had no job, no place to stay, but we began the trek to where God had told us to go. There is so much that could be said of this journey. We traveled through literal ice storms, hail, and torrential rain with three small children. But **as we raised our hands to obey, God provided the way.**

God supernaturally provided a trailer four days before we had to move. Along the way, as I was driving through torrential downpours, I got a call about an interview that I was not really qualified for. God laid it on someone's heart that we did not even know to provide a place for us to stay.

Even during this confirmation and provision, the whole time I felt like I was walking into the sea. It is a good thing God made me hard-headed, because I felt it was being used as a battering ram to break open the way through for my family. It really was six months of laboring to enter into the rest. Going up the mountain to gain the strength and perseverance that I needed, and going down to beat my head against the wall.

Maybe it is the same for you. You probably do not see the provision or the way through. Just like Moses did not see the Sea part before he raised his hands. They did not see the bread falling from heaven to feed them in the wilderness. They did not see the water flowing from the rock. **They had a word, and as they advanced in obedience to The Word, they gained everything they needed to walk into The Promised Land.**

People of God, you cannot be so afraid of the unknown that you are disobedient to The Word. This is the only reason you would remain in bondage, depression, and death. This is why everything starts with hunger, desire, and the longing to follow the Father's call. A true son will obey The Father's voice even when it does not make sense. If you trust The Father is good and has the best plans for you, you will move forward when He says "*Advance!*"

What was the result of Moses and the people's obedience?

> *"You will bring them [into the land of promise] and plant them on the mountain (Mt. Moriah in Jerusalem) of Your inheritance, The place, O Lord, You have made for Your dwelling [among them], The sanctuary, O Lord, which Your hands have established."*
> *Exodus 15:17*

The enemy that enslaved them for generations was completely destroyed. They were truly able to inherit the Promised Land. They inherited and were planted on The Mountain in The Presence of The Lord. **The Lord led, fed, warmed, shaded, and spoke to them in the middle of the wilderness. They were never alone as long as they continued to walk in The Presence of The Lord.** Enemies came and went, troubles arose and were settled. However, this people got to see and hear The Lord on The Mountain in a way that no one else ever had before.

What is your reward for being obedient to move forward?

The presence of The Lord will be with you! You will slay giants because He will equip you. You will take mountains because He will enable you. You will advance The Kingdom because many others need the same freedom, life, and ability to receive the inheritance that you are beginning to walk in as a son.

Many times, you may have the wrong perspective. You are easily able to see what is happening in the physical, but it is time to rise above and begin to see with spiritual eyes. **There can never be a peaceful coex-**

istence with evil. The enemy will always be trying to subvert and pervert if not outright attack The Kingdom. If you sit back and play nice, you will be overcome. **Kingdom advancement is the only way for the people of God to become the sons that inherit the promise.** Complacent Christianity cannot inherit The Kingdom.

Jesus says it this way:

> *"And from the days of John the Baptist until now the kingdom of heaven suffers violence, and the violent take it by force."*
> *Matthew 11:12* (NKJV)

The enemy will always be trying to steal, kill, and destroy whether openly or in the darkness. He does not stop because you do not see or recognize it. However, **light will always dominate darkness. It is time to shine brighter than ever before.** The harshness of a bright light after someone has been in the dark for so long may seem painful for a time, but sight is better than blindness. The most horrendous acts take place in darkness behind closed doors. It is time for The Kingdom to be advanced and totally take over every place that the imposter has illegally ruled for far too long.

We, the people of God, will no longer make excuses saying, a place or people is too hard, too dark, too remote, or impossible to reach. **We will walk through the valley of the shadow of death and bring the light of life that dispels every dark enemy and ruler.** Each one of us will press forward and advance The Kingdom!!!

People are in bondage, lost in the wilderness, and crying out for freedom and deliverance from the darkness and death that has enslaved and blinded them. We are the light bearers, The Kingdom Carriers that have access to everything they need. **We must never hold back or hold in the power that we possess.** We will release The Kingdom wherever The King may take us!!!

In *1 Samuel 14*, there is a picture of the true warrior that advances The Kingdom. Jonathan was the warrior that had led his men into former battles. He had a sword at a time that very few had access to such weapons (see chap *13:19-22*).

He decides one day to go down and attack the Philistine garrison. This host of enemy that is barricaded in their garrison are inhabiting the land given to Israel. Jonathan's armor bearer sees the faith Jonathan has in God and partners with his faith. The fearful King Saul and six hundred men are so consumed with their own comfort, they were sitting under a pomegranate tree, that they do not even know that Jonathan went out.

The warrior, Jonathan, goes to the enemy illegally inhabiting his inheritance, crawls up a mountain on his hands and knees, takes his sword and begins to slay every enemy that he can see. The camp of the enemy was shaken by this one man who advanced into the enemy camp and began to slaughter the enemy. It takes a while, but finally Saul and the six hundred come to help. After that, those hiding in caves came and began to take back their territory. Even those who had been allied with the enemy began to understand the importance of taking back their land and follow Jonathan's lead.

The great victory that came about that day was because one Kingdom-minded son with a sword, was not satisfied with the way things were. He stood up and began to advance The Kingdom with what he had and with whomever would come along with him. **He did not look at the size of the enemy, the strength of the stronghold, or the difficulty it would take to even advance to where the enemy was. He was focused on the faithfulness of God and The Kingdom that lay before him.**

How much more should we as sons be focused on The King and The Kingdom He has placed within our grasp? It is time to reach up and take hold of what you have been given and keep pressing forward.

> *"From that time Jesus began to preach and say, 'Repent [change your inner self—your old way of thinking, regret past sins, live your life in a way that proves repentance; seek God's purpose for your life], for the kingdom of heaven is at hand.'"*
> *Matthew 4:17*

Because of Jesus, The Kingdom is now literally waiting for you to take hold of. It is right here for the taking. Nothing is off limits to the son. Everything that The King has is yours. Ask for it, search it out, grab hold of your inheritance. You do not have because you have not asked, or because you have asked to advance your own kingdom or the kingdom of men.

From the beginning of time, there have been two kingdoms competing. There is no real competition. **The Maker of the Universe is The King of Kings.** However the struggle is who will rule on the earth. The command was given to man to rule the earth, but the enemy came to take away what he has been given. **This struggle is between the advancement of The Kingdom of God and the kingdom of man and his selfish desires and lusts.** This was represented in the Old Testament by baal and various other false idols. Some of the kings of the earth even exalted themselves to the place of a god, like the pharaohs or Nebuchadnezzar.

However, these were humbled in different ways and proven that their temporary power would never overcome The King of Kings. He sits and laughs at their insignificant attempts to overcome the Lord of Hosts. **The King dominates ever other kingdom and has given that same power and authority to His sons.** Those who walk in The Way have complete and total access to The King and all His unlimited resources. These sons are the ones who will rule and reign with Him forever. **It is time to step up into your position as a son and advance The Kingdom of God in every area!**

It should be an encouragement to you that the strongest, fastest, and best do not always win. **The overcomer is the one who wants it more.**

If you remember the story from before, I was about eight years old when I began taking Judo. I had been taking this for about six weeks when the first opportunity to compete came up. My dad told me several times, "you are new, you just started. You are going to learn. You will not win, but you can learn and grow." I was a white belt and literally knew one throw and one pin. Everyone that I was to compete against was more advanced, knew more, and was better in every way. I was so nervous that I was doing thirty or forty push-ups waiting for my turn to compete. I ended up winning two matches within the first five seconds and another one to take home first. My dad and sensei were both amazed.

I relate this story to illustrate the point. I knew hardly anything and had no experience. I had a swarm of butterflies in the my stomach trying to distract me. My dad gave me some additional advice beyond "you cannot win". He said "It is okay to have butterflies, you just have to make them fly in formation."

You, my friend, have been called to be more than an overcomer. You have been given every spiritual blessing in the heavenly realm. The heart of The Father for salvation, healing, and freedom for all mankind has been placed within you.

How much do you want to do the will of The Father?

How much do you want to advance The Kingdom?

The Kingdom of God will advance in every area. There is no geographical location or impossible condition for the rolling forward of The Promise. I have heard so many excuses, "this place is too hard." "That place is too dark." Or "it is too hard to get to." It is time to change this misconception by proving the power of The Promise in every situation and atmosphere.

*If a place seems too hard, take the word like a hammer and break it open (**Jeremiah 23:29**)!!!*

*Reach out and grab the breaker anointing (**Micah 2:13**)!!!*

*Cry out to the God of the breakthrough (**1 Chronicles 14:11**) and walk with Him into a softer place!!!*

*Break up the hard ground and begin to sow seeds that will bear the fruit of the Kingdom (**Hosea 10:12**)!!!*

There are many temporarily dark places on the earth. They were never destined or designed to remain that way. Jesus said this, *"I am the light of the world. He who follows Me shall not walk in darkness, but have the light of life"* (*John 8:12*). If Jesus is with you wherever you go, it cannot stay dark because He will be radiating out of you.

Here is something else Jesus said *"You are the light of the world"* (**Matthew 5:14**). As you allow the presence of Jesus to fill you completely, you will be the light in a dark place revealing who He is. It is not only who you are, but your calling just as Paul was called, *"...to open their eyes, in order to turn them from darkness to light, and from the power of Satan to God..."* (**Acts 26:18**). There goes the excuse that it is too dark. It is only dark because you are not there, or you are not doing your job of letting your big ol' light shine!

There is another pesky problem that is continually brought up. This place is too remote, these people are too hard to get to. My question is *"For who?"* The majority of unreached peoples are in hard to reach locations. The Kingdom of God has not been advanced in these areas because no one has gone there with the gospel.

If you can get on a plane and fly around the world entirely in two days, why would it be impossible to get to the most remote people with the gospel? Planes, trains, and automobiles are not mentioned in the Bible. However, the church in Acts was known for turning the world upside down (*Acts 17:6*). You have been given the shoes of peace for your feet (*Eph 6:15*), and you need to put your beautiful feet into those good news shoes (*Isa 52:7*).

Not only this, you have been given the power, authority, and command to *"go into all the world"*, to be witnesses to the *"uttermost part of the earth"*, and *"preach the gospel to every creature"*.

So why are we not going?

I am convinced more than ever that our selfishness and creature comforts are what hold us back from going. The enemy knows that one carrier of The Kingdom can take territories and shake nations wherever they go. If he can get you to focus on yourself and your own desires, he can keep you from going around the world and across the street. Good things are not the problem. God "... *satisfies your mouth with good things...*" (*Psalm 103:5*). These are blessings from The Lord. However, when you place your focus on the good things and not on the heart of The Father, you will be off track.

You are called to do the new thing. You are designed to pioneer something the world has never seen before. You are commanded to go to the farthest reaches of the universe and to the neighbor across the street. You are a follower of The One who says "... *I will even make a road in the wilderness And rivers in the desert.*" (*Isa 43:19*). **The conditions of this world do not affect you, because you are from a different Kingdom. You are of The Kingdom of God that rules and reigns over the earth.** You are a son partnering with God to bring His Kingdom "...*on earth as it is in heaven*" (*Matt 6:10*).

You are able, and should be willing, to change the conditions and solve the problems that have been placed in front of past generations. The excuses of the past will no longer prevent the people of God from rolling forward to demolish demonic strongholds, slay savage giants, and obliterate the gates of hell. You are not one who draws back in fear, insecurity, or selfishness to destruction, but you are one who believes to the salvation, deliverance, and healing of the soul and nations for the glory of God (*Heb 10:39*).

It only takes a spark! "*The fields are white with harvest*" (*John 4:35*), just as Jesus said. The stage is set for the sons of God to come on the scene and be the spark, the flame, the ignition for The Kingdom to advance and accelerate in every area. Just as when wood is soaked with an accelerant, the tiniest flame can catch the entire burn pile ablaze. This is the time you are living in. It is time to reach out and take hold of The Kingdom for yourself, your family, and your generation and watch as multitudes erupt into blazing infernos for The Kingdom.

You must not hide your light, but let your light shine no matter what size you think it is. Just as Smokey the Bear has said, "Only you can prevent forest fires!" Do not prevent the fire of The Lord from going forth and setting a region on fire. **Nations and neighbors are waiting for what you have that they may be freed and fired to advance The Kingdom themselves.** The Promised Land is waiting for freed sons to take hold of their inheritance and walk into their promise!

As if I had to expound more on what I have already said here is some truth for you and all those who are advancing The Kingdom:

> *"They shall speak of the glory of Your kingdom And talk of Your power, To make known to the sons of men Your mighty acts And the glorious majesty of Your kingdom. Your kingdom is an everlasting kingdom, And Your dominion endures throughout all generations."*
> *Psalm 145:11-13* (NKJV)

The glory of The Kingdom and the power that you have access to when you walk with the King as a son is unlimited and everlasting. The power and authority that is given to you is not to make you look better, but to take dominion and make known to all those on the earth who The King is. His Kingdom is designed for all to come and be a part and walk as sons if they will proclaim Him as King and walk in The Way. **You have been given an inheritance that is enduring and advancing from one generation to the next.**

> *"There shall be no end to the increase of His government and of peace, [He shall rule] on the throne of David and over his kingdom, To establish it and to uphold it with justice and righteousness From that time forward and forevermore. The zeal of the Lord of hosts will accomplish this."*
> *Isaiah 9:7* (NKJV)

The kingdom of man is short lived, and his rule is waning. The only inheritance that can be offered is paltry compared to the continual increase of the peace and government of The King of the universe. Justice, righteousness, and government of the people is carried out by the sons of the King until His return. Your passion for Him and His Kingdom is what will carry you into eternity with Him. **The heart of the son is for the advancement of His Father's Kingdom.**

> *"See, I have appointed you this day over the nations and over the kingdoms, To uproot and break down, To destroy and to overthrow, To build and to plant."*
> *Jeremiah 1:10*

The sons have been empowered in The Kingdom to initiate a righteous and just rule over territories, regions, nations, and people of the earth. **The dark unrighteousness can never coexist with righteous light bringers.** Dark demonic devices will be destroyed and the enemy tactics turned back on their own heads. Any kingdom that tries to exalt itself above The King of kings will be brought low and decimated before The Throne. **Jesus, The Rock, is the unchanging, ever-expanding foundation that The Kingdom is built upon.** The ever-advancing, ever-increasing Kingdom is yours to build, advance, and carry to the ends of the earth.

> *"In the days of those [final ten] kings the God of heaven will set up a kingdom that will never be destroyed, nor will its sovereignty be left for another people; but it will crush and put an end to all these kingdoms, and it will stand forever. Just as you saw that a stone was cut out of the mountain without hands and that it crushed the iron, the bronze, the clay, the silver and the gold, the great God has revealed to the king what will take place in the future; so the dream is true and its interpretation is trustworthy."*
> *Daniel 2:44-45*

Right now, God is using His people to fulfill this prophecy to Daniel. His Kingdom is the one that will never be destroyed. It is greater than any other Kingdom by far, **and no shaking can break down what God has purposed to build.** The kings of this earth may have had a passing glorious reign, but they have all been brought low and passed away. They will be forgotten in a generation or two. However, you are partnered with The ever-lasting, ever-expanding Kingdom that will never be defeated or destroyed. The enemy will do everything he can to delay, but this is his only play. **You have the ability, empowered by The King, to accelerate the advancement of This Kingdom.** You can sit back, do nothing, and delay the destruction of the enemy, or you can press in and see every dark power overthrown and every prisoner set free. Your love for The Father and the heart for His people will cause you to lay down your life to bring total salvation to all mankind and freedom even to the land itself.

"But the saints (believers) of the Most High [God] will receive the kingdom and possess the kingdom forever, for all ages to come."
Daniel 7:18

"... the kingdom and the dominion and the greatness of all the kingdoms under the whole heaven will be given to the people of the saints (believers) of the Most High; His kingdom will be an everlasting kingdom, and all the dominions will serve and obey Him."
Daniel 7:27

O Saint, it is time to receive and possess. You must accept the gift that has been given to you. A high price was paid, the blood of The Savior. The power and authority were given to you through this sacrifice. The Kingdom is now free for you to reach out and take hold of. You must know your inheritance is what has been given and paid for. All creation has been set free and placed in God's hands. It is time to possess the promise and inheritance from your Father.

This legacy cannot be taken from your hand. It must never be laid down or cast off. You must step up and possess completely everything you have been given. You will not abandon the gift that you have been given. It will not be forgotten or overlooked. You will possess the entirety of The Kingdom and the inheritance that has been bought, paid for, and placed within your grasp.

"And as you go, preach, saying, 'The kingdom of heaven is at hand.'
Heal the sick, raise the dead, cleanse the lepers, cast out demons.

Freely you have received, freely give."
Matthew 10:7-8

As you come to understand the call to an ever-advancing Kingdom, you realize that you are compelled to go. **You must continually take steps to move forward.** Everyone must hear the news of what is taking place at this time. The call is to be a part. The power and authority will be demonstrated as The Kingdom advances unconditionally. Sickness cannot stand, disease cannot compete, even death will never defeat the sons of The Kingdom. **You have the full Kingdom without measure or restriction. The invitation is for you and any who would be a part. You have received unlimited access as have all who will lay hold of it.**

> *"From the days of John the Baptist until now the kingdom of heaven suffers violent assault, and violent men seize it by force [as a precious prize]."*
> *Matthew 11:12*

As much peace as The King brings, the enemy will resist just as violently. Although peaceful, a fierce people will fight for the advancement of The Kingdom. The most peaceful animal will become violent when threatened or robbed of its offspring. *How much more will you, O saint, as you are threatened with the destruction of a generation and people in bondage and not yet in The Kingdom, become aggressive in the total destruction of this enemy?* If the enemy will not release those in bondage, you will take them by force. The enemy must be pushed back and slain that generations may be freed and raised to walk in the presence of a compassionate King.

> *"This good news of the kingdom [the gospel] will be preached throughout the whole world as a testimony to all the nations, and then the end [of the age] will come."*
> *Matthew 24:14*

The advancement of The Kingdom is good news for the whole world. Thick darkness, torment and death has enslaved the world since the fall of man. Illegitimate rulers have inflicted cruel punishment on all of creation. There is no hope for the world or those who live under this tyranny to ever be set free without a revolution of regimes. The Kingdom proclaimed in every area is hope of healing, freedom, and life that cannot come from any other source. The final result will be the complete takeover of The Kingdom of Heaven from the kingdom of darkness. **When all illegitimate rulers are dethroned, decommissioned, and decapitated, this will be the end of the age.**

> *"They preached the good news to that city and made many disciples, then they returned to Lystra and to Iconium and to Antioch, strengthening and establishing the hearts of the disciples; encouraging them to remain firm in the faith, saying, 'It is through many tribulations and hardships that we must enter the kingdom of God.'"*
> **Acts 14:21-22**

When Paul and his team came and were preaching The Kingdom to entire cities, many disciples took hold of what he was saying and began walking in The Way. This was the easy part. Paul took it upon himself to encourage the believers in these cities with the full counsel of the gospel. *"It is through many tribulations and hardships that we must enter the kingdom of God."* This was more than just a mild warning or cautionary command. Just before this, people came, and at Lystra, stoned Paul to death (*v.19*). The resurrected Paul came to believers and was telling them that The Kingdom would roll forward. Walking in The Way may not be as easy as you think, and there may be some trouble. This was a testament to not only the power of God, but an expectation that the advancement of The Kingdom was more important than your life and even your death. God has the power to raise you up even after persecution that He may continue His mighty work. **Hungry disciples, bold burning ones, willing warriors are willing to do what it takes to advance The Kingdom no matter what it may cost them.**

What is the difference between the kingdom of darkness and The Kingdom of Light?

The enemy will enslave and force you to serve him in misery, pain, and death all while building a demonic rulership that will cause destruction in everyone around you. The Kingdom of Light brings freedom and life. You are called to join with the ever-advancing Kingdom and lay down your life that you may be an inheritor and gain full rights as a son to everything in The Kingdom. Your new birth gives you the birthright and everything The Father has is now yours!

> *"For He has rescued us and has drawn us to Himself from the dominion of darkness, and has transferred us to the kingdom of His beloved Son"*
> **Colossians 1:13**

As you turn and come to The Father by the gift given you by the blood of Jesus, you are reborn. What once enslaved has now been broken and made an open display by the blood of Jesus. You have transitioned from death to life and are a son in the Kingdom of Light. The Father is "not willing that any should perish, but all should come to repentance" (*2 Peter 3:9*).

This will become your heart as you come to know Him more. This is the ever-advancing Kingdom. Setting those in bondage free, proclaiming the good news, and demonstrating the heart of The Father. Every son will be set free, every enemy brought into judgment and defeated. He has chosen you to be a part of advancing The Kingdom and receiving this promise to the fullest.

In *Hebrews 12:25-29*, we see the transition to The Unshakeable Kingdom. The Word of God is the enduring promise that propels you into the continually refining of not just your own life but all of creation. Neither this world or anyone in it were designed for destruction. Eternity has been placed here, and the enemy has only perverted and subverted what God has created. Freedom, true life, and eternity will shine forth as every other thing is broken off. The fire of The Word of The Father will burn away every perversion and stronghold of the enemy.

Only The Word that endures will remain and those who are being

molded, shaped, and refined by it. You will lay down the things of yourself that can be held onto from the past, weights that have been placed on you. Temptations that are common to man. This is not who you are. It is never who you were designed to be. These things will be shaken loose and burned up in the holy fire of The Word of The Kingdom. **As you walk into The Eternal Kingdom, you will step forward continually to advance this Kingdom and declare freedom and life to all those living in darkness and bondage.** The gift of grace is for everyone if they will reach out and take it.

> *"Then I heard a loud voice in heaven, saying, 'Now the salvation, and the power, and the kingdom (dominion, reign) of our God, and the authority of His Christ have come; for the accuser of our [believing] brothers and sisters has been thrown down [at last], he who accuses them and keeps bringing charges [of sinful behavior] against them before our God day and night. And they overcame and conquered him because of the blood of the Lamb and because of the word of their testimony, for they did not love their life and renounce their faith even when faced with death.'"*
> **Revelation 12:10-11**

This is how you must position yourself. This is the future of all things being walked out in the day to day. This is how you overcome and walk into The Eternal, Unshakeable Kingdom. This is how the accuser will be thrown down. The age-old liar, deceiver, illegal oppressor will be completely overthrown and cast down. He will not stop his accusations but you will overcome him.

How will you overcome?

The blood of Jesus has paid the price. You have been set completely free and given the power to walk as a son of The King. As you declare the goodness of God and the promise that has been given to you, this testimony will not only cause you to walk in The Way, but will open the door for others to be liberated. It is not only the sacrifice of The King, and The Promise that is spoken, but also the actions that come into line with all these things.

The unyielding will, to carry The Word of promise and advance The Kingdom no matter what, causes you to love just like The Father loved. He sent His Son to lay down His life for you, and you will become willing to lay down your very life so others can receive the inheritance they have been given. In this place, the enemy will already be defeated. Just as Jesus gained the victory both in life and death, whether you live or die, **The Kingdom advances in those whose heart and will has become one with The Father.**

Remaining in this place will position you correctly and will cause your thinking to come into line with Kingdom thinking. As a human, you tend to have highs and lows. You go up the mountain to receive and coast down into the valley and begin to trek back up the mountain again.

In 2012, I got a word about, "The Way Walkers." It was quite simple. We are not the coasting type of community. We are not riding a roller coaster that is subject to the highs and lows of the world, eventually having to get out and push to get back up the mountain. Those walking in The Way are a steam locomotive. We are not affected by the environment around us. We are continually advancing. We may pick up speed or slow at points, but we are endlessly moving forward. The fire of the love of The Lord is within us. As we fuel this fire in intimacy with Him, this will cause the fire to burn brighter in us. The water of The Word of Promise that comes and is placed in this fire does not extinguish it, but gives power to the ever-advancing Kingdom.

We are moving forward with the heart of The Father, in continual intimacy with Him, and in partnership with The Word of Promise. This will cause us both personally and corporately, as we come together with like-minded community, to be ever-advancing, ever-increasing, ever- picking up speed. This is who you are and who you were created to be. Nothing can stop the barrelling freight train of The Kingdom. We have, we are, and we will overcome every enemy and dark kingdom that would stand against The King. This is The Eternal, Unshakable Kingdom that you are a part of. **Now is The Time!!! Let's Go!!!**

CHAPTER 9

CONCLUSION

ALL PEOPLE EVERYWHERE will walk through a wilderness. This will look different for each person, but the wilderness is still there. **The people of God, who know they are sons and inheritors of The Promise, will be led through the wilderness to be refined and made strong and come out as bright, shining, superabundant conquerors.** This is who you and I are called to be!

> "Do you not know that the unrighteous will not inherit or have any share in the kingdom of God?..."
> *1 Corinthians 6:9*

You and I are being transformed into the righteousness of God even though we are already made that way positionally (*2 Cor 5:21*). In the wilderness, your mind, will, emotions, are being tested, tried, and purified. This can be described as unpleasant, uncomfortable, and even painful at times. Normal people do not enjoy the refining, but they celebrate the result on the other side. **The fullness of The Promise is on the other side of the wilderness if we do not quit, back down, or turn back.** We must continually press in to Jesus the One who started us on this journey. He is with us to the very end of this age and throughout eternity.

The Promised Land was what kept the former slaves of Israel continually moving through the wilderness. Initially, they rejected The Promise because they were afraid of the giants.

Is it possible that this was not the only promise they rejected because their minds had not yet been transformed into that of sons and inheritors?

In the wilderness, there is another opportunity for them to step into a greater promise and inheritance than that of the physical land of possession.

Just as God had spoken to Moses from the burning bush, He led His people out of bondage into the wilderness. They returned to the very same mountain to worship God. While here, God speaks to them the ten commandments. Immediately following this, both in *Exodus* and *Deuteronomy* an interesting event takes place:

> *"The Lord spoke with you face to face at the mountain from the midst of the fire..."*
> **Deuteronomy 5:4**

The Creator of the Universe does not just give the ten commandments to Moses, but He comes and speaks to the people personally.
How can we comprehend the totality of what was taking place?

God had revealed and spoken to individuals before this, but never to an entire congregation such as this. **Here was their opportunity to have full and complete communion with God. There were no obstructions, no ceremonies, no limitations placed on them** beyond the process of purification they had all been through.

Moses had been here before, face to face with God in the burning bush. It was slightly different because The Presence of The Lord now inhabited not just a bush, but the entire mountain.

> *"Now all the people witnessed the thunder and the flashes of lightning and the sound of the trumpet and the smoking mountain..."*
> **Exodus 20:18**

There was no doubt for anyone that this was where God was. They heard God thunder, trumpet, and speak the words of the covenant. They saw the flashes of lightning and fire on The Mountain. The smell of the smoke and taste of it was in their mouths. This was the same God who had plagued the Egyptians, parted the Sea, and protected these people in every possible way. **This was their opportunity to step up into being true sons and inheritors,** not of a physical land, but **of an eternal God and Kingdom that would never be shaken.** This was the place to encounter God and be changed into His image.

Their response is much the same as ours, if we were to be honest.

> *"...and as they looked, the people were afraid, and they trembled [and moved backward] and stood at a [safe] distance. Then they said to Moses, 'You speak to us and we will listen, but do not let God speak to us or we will die.'"*
> *Exodus 20:18-19*

The people had been raised in a fearful, religious mentality. God was supernaturally distant and far off. They were supposed to pray the prayers and make sacrifices but never speak to Him or hear His Word. When God revealed Himself and began to speak The Word that would bring change and reveal identity, they moved away. **They did not want the change of thought, action, and lifestyle that the fire would bring.** Their identity was wrapped up in what they saw and knew. The fire of The Word was uncomfortable, unpleasant, and even painful. They did not want to let go of false mentalities and mindsets. **In rejecting The Word, they rejected the very presence of God.** They rejected the heavenly identity that God was speaking that they might ascend The Mountain and commune with Him. **Ruling and reigning is only for those who know they are sons.** Walking in the slave mentality, they knew this is not what they deserved and could not move past this bondage of the mind.

They rejected The Word that would bring change and thus rejected the blessing of communing with God face to face.

How many times do we do this in our own lives?

A word comes forth and we say that it is for someone else. God calls us to step out in obedience, but we make excuses why we cannot do that right now. **The Word will change us if we allow it to purify, refine, and reveal. The point of the fiery Word of The Father is to bring us into closer relationship as sons and cause us to step up more in being the inheritors that we were designed to be.**

Moses had been here before. He knew the cost, the refining, and the result. **He knew that whatever part of him that needed to die to get closer to The Presence, it was worth it.** This was his response:

> *"Moses said to the people, 'Do not be afraid; for God has come in order to test you, and in order that the fear of Him [that is, a profound reverence for Him] will remain with you, so that you do not sin.' So the people stood at a [safe] distance, but Moses approached the thick cloud where God was."*
> *Exodus 20:20-21*

The people stood a safe distance away from the fire, The Word, and the presence. They were close enough to see but not close enough to be changed. **Moses knew that the closer he could go, the better it would be. Even if his flesh had to die, it was worth it to walk more into his identity as a son.** Moses went into the cloud, the very Presence of God. He drew near. Even though Moses never stepped into the physical promised land because of what would happen later, **at this moment, he stepped into the fullness of the heavenly promise.**

A son is not afraid to come close to his father. Even when a father is angry or has to discipline his son, a son is not afraid to draw near to his good father. Moses knew this, and He stepped into something that no one else would. Later we see that God spoke to Moses face to face as with a friend. *Why?* Because he was not afraid to come close. The writings and words were given to Moses, and Moses gave it to the people. It was easier to receive secondarily, and easier to ignore, when it came from a messenger rather than the mouth of The Author.

"The Lord spoke these words with a great voice to all your assembly at the mountain out of the midst of the fire, the cloud, and the thick darkness, and He added no more. He wrote these commandments on two tablets of stone and gave them to me."
Deuteronomy 5:4,22

God stopped speaking to the people because they no longer desired to come close to Him. His words are for those who will come close, obey, and be changed more and more into sons. The farther you are away, and the less you desire to be with God, the less you will be able to receive. **It is time to come close, and step into The Presence no matter what things of this world that you have to give up!**
Hebrews 11 is known as, "The Faith Chapter." All throughout this chapter great men of faith are named and celebrated. These are heroes that have walked close to God, in spite of their failures, and have stepped into their identity as sons. **They gave up and stepped out of the mentality of the flesh and bondage and put on the identity of a son.** This change came as they heard and obeyed the very voice of God. If we look at the results we desire these things:

"by faith [that is, with an enduring trust in God and His promises] subdued kingdoms, administered justice, obtained promised blessings, closed the mouths of lions, extinguished the power of [raging] fire, escaped the edge of the sword, out of weakness were made strong, became mighty and unbeatable in battle, putting enemy forces to flight. Women received back their dead by resurrection..."
Hebrews 11:33-35

We desire to see these things manifest in our lives. We want the benefits without the cost. We want the Promised Land without the wilderness. We want the result without the process. We want the inheritance without walking as a son.

What was the process to receive these things?

> *"... others were tortured [to death], refusing to accept release*
> *[offered on the condition of denying their faith], so that they would*
> *be resurrected to a better life; and others experienced the trial*
> *of mocking and scourging [amid torture], and even chains and*
> *imprisonment. They were stoned [to death], they were sawn in two,*
> *they were lured with tempting offers [to renounce their faith], they*
> *were put to death by the sword; they went about wrapped in the*
> *skins of sheep and goats, utterly destitute, oppressed, cruelly treated*
> *(people of whom the world was not worthy), wandering in deserts*
> *and mountains and [living in] caves and holes in the ground."*
> *Hebrews 11:35-38*

The inheritors were not appreciated or received. **The slaves were, and still are, constantly at enmity with the sons.** They went through great trials, tribulations, and tests that they might receive a promise. **Right now, we have received this promise. We are able to come as close as we want to The Fire, The Presence, The Promise.** God is continually speaking to us. Let this be an encouragement:

> *"See to it that you do not refuse [to listen to] Him who is speaking*
> *[to you now]..."*
> *Hebrews 12:25*

Right here, right now, God is speaking to you. Throughout this book, I have not been laying out a theoretical concept for some super holy people to begin walking in for anyone else but you. **You are designed to be a son and inheritor in The Kingdom! You are designed to be in a close relationship with The Good Father!**
Everything in this book has been written that you would be able to step fully into it. If you have read this far, it is evident that you are hungry and desire something more. The slave mentality is being broken off of you even as The Word of Promise has been continually spoken over you. **Do not reject or refuse this invitation to come close. It is time for you to rise up!**

In the middle of a generation of people that have submitted themselves to the ways of the world and settled for less than the fullness of The Promise of the eternally advancing Kingdom, **you are being called out.** You have received and read this book for a reason. Somehow, in some way, you have not only gotten ahold of this book but have continued to the very end. **Now is your time of decision.** The people had a decision to make at the mountain, *would they listen to The Word? Would they begin to walk in obedience into a closer relationship with The Lord?*

Will you?

Will you walk into the fullness?

Will you become a son and inheritor?

Now is The Time!!!

The final thought I want to leave with you is this, Peter was a hard-headed, prideful, outspoken person with many problems. He was not intelligent in the world or in the things of the Spirit. He was a lost, hurting and broken man. However, he chose to follow Jesus and come close to Him. Peter was in the middle of a wilderness when he thought he was going to die in a boat in the storm.

How much more did this fear of death come when Jesus told him to come out on the water in the raging storm?

Peter was afraid, but somehow he knew that if Jesus called him to come, he would be safe. He got out of the boat and walked on the water to Jesus. **Yes, he fell along the way. He did not do it right. He had to cry out for help, but he walked in the presence of Jesus in a way no one ever had before.** Jesus did not let him drown to teach him a lesson. Jesus raised him up and walked with him until he was able to walk on his own.

The enemy will try to discourage you, bring you down, or cause you to quit because of any supposed failure. Did Peter fail? No, he walked on the water. Later, he would be brought before the most respected religious leaders of the time and cause them to shut their mouths at the wisdom he was speaking. They realized that he had been with Jesus (*Acts 4:13*), and this is what made the difference in his life.

Wherever you may be, whatever you may be going through, it is time to rise up and go to the next level.

How do you do this?

It is time for you to come out of the world and be with Jesus. **This is your first step walking in The Wilderness Way!!!**

ABOUT THE AUTHOR

JEREMIAH GIBSON is a man who has said "Yes" to The Lord in every area of his life. He is a diligent disciple, humble husband, faithful father, and "Man on Fire". Jeremiah and his wife Katie are called to lead people out of bondage to the place of encounter by advancing The Truth. They do this by focusing on: raising hungry hearts, training burning ones, and arming warriors to slay giants, take mountains and advance The Kingdom.

ENDNOTE

1. (https://www.abarim-publications.com/Dictionary/d/d-b-r.html)

RECOMMENDED BOOKS BY JEREMIAH GIBSON

WHAT'S THe 40 ALL ABOUT?

"LONG AGO, IN THE AGES OF HISTORY, A RELIC WAS DISCOVERED AND UTILIZED TO PROPEL ITS USERS INTO GREATER, DEEPER, MORE POWERFUL AND INTIMATE TIMES WITH THE LORD. ONCE DISCOVERED AND APPLIED, THIS PRIZE HAS LITERALLY CHANGED THE COURSE OF NOT ONLY INDIVIDUALS, BUT ENTIRE NATIONS AND EVEN GENERATIONS..."

CONTRIBUTING AUTHOR

DOXOLOGY IS A COLLECTION OF SONGS, PSALMS, AND POEMS.

THE CHRIST COLLECTIVE IS A TIMELESS COLLECTION OF WRITINGS FROM BELIEVERS AROUND THE WORLD, ALL POINTING TO ONE PERSON: JESUS.

CONTACT

 GIBSONSGOGLOBAL.COM